THE
Kate Greenaway
·DOLL·BOOK·

THE
Kate Greenaway
·DOLL·BOOK·

VALERIE JANITCH

A David & Charles Craft Book

– ACKNOWLEDGEMENTS –

Special thanks must go to Rob Matheson for his photography. My thanks also to Eve Williams and Michael Kinnane of Preston Library, Wembley for their enthusiastic help in tracing all the Kate Greenaway illustrated material on which the designs in this book are based. Also to the Kate Greenaway Collection, Keats House, London for their kind permission to use the Kate Greenaway original illustrations – and to Judith Knight for her patient assistance.

British Library Cataloguing in Publication Data

Janitch, Valerie
    The Kate Greenaway doll book.
    1. Dollmaking   2. Doll clothes
    I. Title
    745.592'21   TT175

    ISBN 0-7153-8976-9

Design by Grub Street Design, London
Typeset by Typesetters (Birmingham) Ltd,
Smethwick, West Midlands
Printed in West Germany
by Mohndruck GmbH
for David & Charles Publishers plc
Brunel House   Newton Abbot   Devon

Distributed in the United States by
Sterling Publishing Co, Inc,
2 Park Avenue, New York, NY 10016

THE CHARM OF KATE GREENAWAY

Who was Kate Greenaway?

A century ago the name Kate Greenaway was a household word. She was a brilliant artist who sought, and found, beauty in almost everything; indeed, she sometimes worried because she saw so little around her that was bad or ugly. She had a very special talent: she could capture and convey this rose-tinted view of life and nature to others. And today her work is still known and appreciated around the world.

As a child she loved dolls, and couldn't wait to spend her weekly farthing on another doll to add to her cherished collection. Then she would be absorbed for hours, dressing them in bits of fabric and trimming she could find around the home or beg from her mother's fancy goods shop. The enchanted world of childhood make-believe never left her. And as her talent developed, it emerged from her drawing board in the sensitive studies of young people which made her a best-selling illustrator of children's books.

Her drawings of both children and flowers were tender and touching, carefully observed and beautifully executed. Her use of colour was fresh and subtle, in gentle contrast to the oppressive drapery and dark clothes of the period.

She became the darling of the late Victorians. They couldn't get enough of her enchanting children, elegantly dressed young ladies and delicate flower studies: each new illustrated book was eagerly awaited and discussed. Her work was so fresh and natural that it came as a breath of fresh air to the rather stuffy, straight-laced society of the 1880s.

Her characters were not overdressed in the stiff, uncomfortable styles of the late nineteenth century. Instead, she looked back to the very early years of the century for inspiration, and so popular were her imaginative drawings of girls, wearing simple, loosely gathered dresses in which they could move freely and gracefully, that they themselves set a fashion.

All the dolls in this book were inspired by the characters in Kate Greenaway's illustrations. They are wearing the charming, high-waisted dresses and big bonnets that so delighted the Victorians, reminding them of the old-fashioned styles worn by their own great-grandmothers.

CONTENTS

CHAPTER 1

WHAT IS THE KATE GREENAWAY DOLL?

Who can make it?   9
The Kate Greenaway designer label   9
Copyright   9

CHAPTER 2

BEFORE YOU BEGIN: TIPS AND TECHNIQUES

Equipment and materials   10
Guidelines   11
Ribbon bows   15
Plaited braid   16
Satin roses   17
If this is your very first doll   18

CHAPTER 3

THE KATE GREENAWAY DOLL

How to make the basic doll   19
Hairstyles   21
Features   23

CHAPTER 4

UP WITH THE LARK

Emily's Chemise and Pantalettes   24
Charlotte's Chemise and Pantalettes   28
Louisa's Chemise and Pantalettes 28
Mary-Anne's Camisole, Petticoat
   and Pantalettes 29
Shoes, Pumps and Slippers 30

CHAPTER 5

BIRTHDAY BREAKFAST

Charlotte's Dark Flowered Dress   31
Charlotte's Spotted Voile Pinafore   33
Charlotte's Matching Mob Cap   33
Louisa's Almond Green Braided Dress   36
Louisa's Apron and Mob Cap   38
Mary-Anne's Lace-trimmed Brown Dress   38
Mary-Anne's Shawl Collar and Mob Cap   40
Emily's Yellow Rose Print Dress   40
Emily's Filmy Stole and Mob Cap   42
Louisa's Birthday Doll   43

CHAPTER 6

IMPROVING OCCUPATIONS

Four variations on the basic shift dress   47

CHAPTER 7

GOING SHOPPING

Louisa's Sprigged White Dress   48
Louisa's Frilly Shoulder Cape   48
Louisa's Wide-brimmed Hat   51
Mary-Anne's Brown Sprigged Dress   52
Mary-Anne's Spencer Jacket   52
Mary-Anne's Brown Sprigged Bonnet   54
Louisa and Mary-Anne's Purses   54
Mary-Anne's Shopping Basket   55

CHAPTER 8

SUMMER GARDEN PARTY

Emily's Lilac and Tartan Dress and
   Matching Bonnet   56
Emily's Tasselled Purse   61

Mary-Anne's Garden Party Dress   61
Mary-Anne's Picture Hat, Parasol and
   Stole   63

CHAPTER 9

WINTER VISITING

Louisa's Olive Green Cloak   66
Louisa's Matching Bonnet and Muff   69
Charlotte's Violet Coat   70
Charlotte's Matching Hat and Muff   71

CHAPTER 10

PARTY-GOING

Emily's Old-fashioned Ballgown   75

CHAPTER 11

TIME FOR BED

Charlotte's Lovers' Knots and Lace
   Négligé   78
Louisa's Frilly Summer Nightgown and
   Matching Nightcap   82
Emily's Warm Winter Nightgown and
   Matching Nightcap   84

CHAPTER 12

WILLIAM, THE GREENAWAY GIRLS' HOUND

William   86
William's Winter Jacket   88
William's Nightcap   88

CHAPTER 13

THE GREENAWAY GIRLS' FURNITURE   89

Making cylindrical bases for the furniture   90
Birthday Breakfast Table and Stools   90

Velvet Upholstered Chair   91
Matching Padded Footstool   94
Round Cushion   94
Small Side Table with Fringed Cloth   95
Flowery Triple-folding Screen   95
Fairytale Ribbon and Roses Four-poster
   Bed   96
Rosebud and Ribbons Bedroom Table   100
Roses and Lace Kidney-shaped Dressing
   Table   101
Dressing Table Stool   104
Pearl-framed Dressing Table Mirror   105
Powder-puff and Pincushion   106
Curtained Wardrobe with Bottom Drawer   107
Covered Hangers   108

CHAPTER 14

SELLING YOUR KATE GREENAWAY DOLLS

Market research   111
What kind of doll?   112
Plan ahead for Christmas   112
Shopping around   112
Getting down to work   113
An eye on the clock   113
'Mini' mass-production   114
Presentation   114
Pricing, tax and publicity   115
The Kate Greenaway doll designer labels   115

CHAPTER 15

Recommended Stockists and Suppliers   116

CHAPTER 1

WHAT IS THE KATE GREENAWAY DOLL?

The Kate Greenaway doll is made of felt which means that it is *very* simple to make. It is easy to cut out, the edges are oversewn, there are no awkward turnings, no seams to fray, and it stuffs well. The size – 40cm (16in) – is designed to be practical: large enough to prevent dressing becoming fiddly, but small enough to avoid long, boring seams when making the clothes – in fact, just the right size for a small child to cuddle or to sit on your bed looking pretty.

The Kate Greenaway doll has a slim figure to show off the high-waisted, Kate Greenaway-style dresses: her limbs move and bend easily, so the doll will sit comfortably and move naturally. Her features are deliberately simple – with no complicated embroidery – to ensure that *your* doll is as demurely pretty as those illustrated in this book. Her hair is knitting yarn in a choice of several attractive styles, all variations of a very straightforward basic method.

The patterns for the doll and her extensive wardrobe given in this book are actual-size, so you don't have to do any laborious redrawing to scale them up. All the materials required are listed in full at the outset, so you can see exactly what you will need, and you can either follow the colour schemes of the examples illustrated or design your own.

And when you've made the doll and all the outfits she needs, you can furnish her home. The furniture is just as easy to make as the doll and her clothes, and it's all based on throwaway cartons, cereal packets and scrap paper. So if you think it's all a lot of rubbish – you're very nearly right!

WHO CAN MAKE IT?

The Kate Greenaway doll is special because she is designed for *everyone* who has ever wanted to make a doll – or wondered if they could make one – or perhaps hasn't even thought about it till now! Whether you have never made a doll before or whether you have made hundreds, whether you are eight years old or eighty, if you can sew, you can make the Kate Greenaway doll and be proud of the result.

Everything about the doll and her wardrobe is designed to be as simple, quick and easy to make as possible. Added to this, the directions explain every stage fully, with diagrams to help, so you are taken step by step from the first move through to the finished article. If you are a veteran doll-maker, you'll probably be happy to skip the instructions for operations with which you are already familiar. But it's all there if you need it. If you *haven't* made a doll before, there's a special introductory section in chapter 2 to start you off confidently and happily.

THE KATE GREENAWAY
DESIGNER LABEL

The Kate Greenaway designer label is unique. It makes your doll into something extra-special. It shows that she is your own creation and very individual. It identifies *your* doll and proves that *you* made it.

If you make the doll for yourself, or as a gift, she will wear her label with pride, proclaiming to everyone how clever you are! But if you are planning to sell your dolls, the Kate Greenaway label is even more important. It gives your work a strictly professional quality: it not only identifies the doll, emphasising all the romantic nostalgia evoked by the name Kate Greenaway, it is also a hallmark of the high standard of workmanship that you put into the creation of every doll you produce. Simply fill in the name you have chosen for your doll (which will immediately give her a character of her own), followed by where she was made and your own name. Then stick the label onto a stiff card backing.

The Kate Greenaway designer label takes the word 'amateur' out of doll-making. It means that you can compete on equal terms with any other doll-producer. Look in the shops and compare your dolls with all the others: if your standard is as good as the best and better than the rest, then you are a true professional and your work *deserves* the Kate Greenaway designer label. Your Kate Greenaway labels, all ready for use, can be found at the end of the book. Additional labels are available on request: please see chapter 14 for details.

COPYRIGHT

Unlike most craft publications, there are no copyright restrictions on the designs in this book, as long as you are planning to produce the dolls personally, and therefore in limited numbers. *The Kate Greenaway Doll Book* is an answer to all those people who have written to me to say that they would like to sell their work and have asked permission to use my designs for this purpose.

The doll is specially designed to be quick, easy and inexpensive to make: which is, of course, just what you are looking for if you are planning to sell her. And she's all yours – *without* the asking!

CHAPTER 2

BEFORE YOU BEGIN: TIPS AND TECHNIQUES

I f you have never made a doll before, take care to read *all* this chapter before you begin. It explains how to choose your materials and what equipment you will need. The Guidelines are important too, so read through these carefully, but there's no need to try to remember everything. Once you know they are there, you can turn back to look up what you need to know – when you need to know it. After this you'll be anxious to begin – so there's a special section just for you, to start you off along the right lines and ensure that your very first doll will win admiring compliments from all who meet her.

Nearly everyone knows a special little girl who deserves a very special present. And if you're going to spoil her, you might as well do it properly! An enchanting doll in a smart outfit, complete with dainty underpinnings and frilly mob cap or demure bonnet, makes a lovely gift to win the heart of any small girl. But imagine her face if her new moppet has her own curtained four-poster bed or draped dressing table trimmed with lace and roses – *that* would make your present *very* special!

If you want to sell your work, however, you will be looking for profit from designs that are quick, easy and inexpensive to produce, designs that you can adapt and alter to make your work even more individual – and look so good it merits a worthwhile price tag – and a finished product that is so attractive, your customers will be queueing up to buy

your work. The Kate Greenaway doll offers you all that. And more. There's the authentic Kate Greenaway designer label to make sure everyone knows all about your dolls, and who made them. And a final bonus: there's a special section at the end of the book packed with useful advice to help you plan, organise, cost and set up the operation in a businesslike way, plus hints on buying materials, adapting designs, saving time, 'mini' mass-production, packaging and finding the right market for you.

EQUIPMENT AND MATERIALS

You will need only the most basic sewing equipment to make and dress your Kate Greenaway doll. But make sure that your needles have sharp points: blunt or bent pins and needles make sewing difficult. And your scissors should be well aligned and sharp: try to have one pair for cutting out and a smaller, pointed pair for all the sewing jobs. You'll need two very tiny safety-pins, a long darning needle and a large tapestry needle. Although you *can* manage without pinking shears, they are a great help: so if you haven't any, try to borrow a pair.

You will also need tracing paper (household greaseproof paper is quite good enough), a well-sharpened pencil and a ruler for tracing the patterns. All pattern pieces are shown in a darker colour to differentiate them from diagrams. A pair of compasses is a great help, though not essential. Skirts and

other straightforward shapes are shown as diagrams, and all you have to do is draw a rectangle to the measurements given. You will find it helpful to have a large sheet of graph paper (or rule a squared sheet yourself) over which you can place your tracing paper to measure out the pattern and draw the lines with a ruler. A separate pair of scissors for cutting out your paper patterns will save you blunting your needlework scissors. A sharp craft knife is essential to cut the board and card for the furniture. Always use it with a metal-edge rule.

The most suitable type of fabric is recommended for each outfit, and if you keep fairly close to this, you can be sure of a good result. You will find some additional notes on the fabrics used for the dolls in the Guidelines that follow. Trimmings are also described in detail in the lists of materials. Look out for pretty lace edgings and narrow braids. And you can make you own trimmings, too: instructions for making plaited braid, satin roses and two ways to make bows are given later in this chapter.

Glue is important: you will often need it to fix trimmings or hold fabrics down. Use it very sparingly on fabric, a little at a time. More information on adhesives is given in the following Guidelines.

Nearly all the outfits, and also the furniture, are enhanced by ribbon trimmings in shades to match, tone or contrast. Offray produces a wide selection of ribbons in a wonderful range of colours, so you can be sure the ones you choose are exactly right for your doll or the piece of furniture you are trimming.

GUIDELINES

FOLLOWING THE DIRECTIONS: The instructions are numbered step by step, and it is always a good idea to read through the *whole* of each step, even though it may contain several operations. This will give you a clear picture of what you are aiming to achieve at each stage, which will make it easier to understand each part of it.

FABRICS: You will always find an indication of the most suitable type of fabric to use for the garment or piece of furniture you are planning to make. It is important to avoid thick or knobbly fabrics, which are too bulky for items on such a small scale: you will find them difficult to work with, and the results will be disappointing.

The other point to watch for is a firm, close weave: loosely woven fabrics are difficult to work with because they fray easily. You will soon find yourself in trouble if you try to sew small pieces with tiny seams which immediately begin to fray. If you are specially keen to use a loosely woven fabric, have a look at Emily's Ballgown in chapter 10. In this case, the satin (which also tends to fray) is backed with a very fine, iron-on interlining, which prevents this happening. So if you can't avoid using a loose weave, this is the best way to solve the problem. However, it will also stiffen the fabric, so bear this in mind if you want a softly gathered effect.

When a medium-weight fabric is recommended, choose a firmly woven cotton-type fabric, like a poplin or polyester-blend summer dress material. If you have difficulty finding pretty sprigged cottons in the dress fabric department, try cotton sheeting: it's a good weight for the Kate Greenaway dresses, and the designs are often perfect – as you can see when Louisa and Mary-Anne go shopping in chapter 7.

You will notice that several of the garments, and all the underwear, are made of spotted voile. This is another ideal fabric for the Kate Greenaway styles: it is soft and fine, and the dainty flock spots make it very pretty, but it is firmly woven and easy to sew. It has another advantage, too: it allows you to 'cheat'. When you have to cut a straight line, you can follow the spots!

FELT: It is important to use good-quality felt, especially for the doll itself. It should be smooth and firm, neither too thick nor too thin, but an even thickness all over. Poor-quality felt is difficult to work with, and gives unsatisfactory results, as your stitches will pull away when any strain is put on them. For the doll, it is wise to pin all your pattern pieces in the *same* direction as there is a certain amount of stretch in most felts, and this may cause problems when the limbs are stuffed.

TRACING PATTERNS: Trace all patterns onto household greaseproof paper, or non-woven interlining (Vilene) if you intend to use them often. For greatest accuracy when cutting small pieces, trace those patterns with a FOLD onto *folded* paper (or interlining): cut through the double thickness, then open out to cut flat in single fabric or felt. Trace all notches and similar markings, then transfer them to the *wrong* side of each piece of fabric or felt when you have cut them out.

For patterns that are to be cut in thin card or paper (bonnets, hats, etc), trace the patterns first onto greaseproof paper, then transfer to the card. To do this, rub over the back of the tracing paper with a soft pencil, then place this side flat on your card (taping down, if necessary, to prevent the trace moving) and go over the lines with a firm point (ballpoint pen, hard pencil or fine knitting needle). When you remove the trace, a clear outline should remain on the card. (For patterns that are traced onto folded paper, turn the tracing over and trace your original outline through onto the other side before opening it up: then transfer the complete shape to the card.)

Patterns are always given in the book for you to trace the circular pieces for bonnets, hats, etc, which are to be cut in either paper or card. But if you have a pair of compasses, *do* use them to draw the circles, measuring the radius against the pattern. This ensures absolute accuracy and is much quicker too!

CUTTING FABRIC: Pattern pieces are placed across the width of the fabric for cutting, so that if you are buying fabric, you will need to purchase the smallest possible amount. But in case you are using a piece of fabric you already have, the width quoted in the list of materials is not always an accepted loom width from selvedge to selvedge, but indicates the actual width of fabric needed.

ARROWS (ON FABRIC): Arrows indicate the straight grain of the fabric, ie the 'up and down' of the weave: the arrow should be parallel to the selvedge when the pattern is placed on the fabric. Felt pieces may be cut in any direction (but note special instructions when making the doll: see chapter 3).

CUTTING OUT – REVERSING PATTERNS: When a pattern piece is marked 'reverse', it means that you must turn the pattern over to cut the second piece. As these two pieces will always meet at the centre, cut them side by side, and check to make sure that any pattern on the fabric falls in the same position on both pieces. Or you could cut the two pieces together in folded double fabric, with the fold on either the left- or right-hand side of the pattern.

MATCHING NOTCHES: Always mark notches on the *wrong* side of the fabric. When notches are to be matched (especially if one side of the fabric or felt is gathered, as in the case of the doll's head, or when joining a skirt to the bodice), it is helpful to mark each notch on one of the pieces (the gathered side) with a pin just before you begin that operation, so that the heads extend beyond the edge of the fabric: then you can line up each notch on the other side under a pin-head.

CUTTING TINY CIRCLES (IN FELT): It is not easy to cut a very small circle round a paper pattern, so here is a useful way to overcome the problem by marking the

circle directly onto the felt. Find something with a circular rim the size you require: it might be a thimble, the top from a bottle or tube, the cap off a pen or something similar – but the sharper the edge of the rim, the better. Using a contrasting colour, rub a wax crayon, lead pencil, felt-tip pen or piece of chalk liberally over the rim. Press the object down hard onto the felt: then, still pressing down very firmly, twist it, taking great care not to move the position – just as you would with a pastry cutter to make biscuits or cookies! Lift off, and a clear impression should remain on the felt. Cut along the marked line with small, sharp scissors.

SEAMS: 3mm (⅛in) seams are allowed on fabrics. To join felt, oversew the edges. Work with the right sides together, unless otherwise stated.

SEWING THREAD: For all the items in the book, use your favourite brand of regular sewing thread in the strength recommended for medium-weight fabrics, matching the colour as closely as possible. Drawing your thread through a block of beeswax before you begin sewing makes it much stronger, and less likely to knot or tangle. When sewing by hand, use a fairly fine needle.

HAIR: Thick knitting yarn is used for all the hairstyles. Any very thick yarn in a suitable shade will do (wool is fluffier and more 'natural' than synthetic, but man-made fibres are quite satisfactory). As a guide, the yarns used for the dolls illustrated are: Emu Aran for Louisa, and Paton's Capstan for the others.

ELASTIC: Buy the narrowest round elastic available (not shirring elastic, except where specified), and use a tiny safety-pin to thread it through narrow hems for sleeves, waists, mob caps, etc. Fix another safety-pin to the other end to prevent it disappearing!

RIBBONS: All the ribbons used for these designs are by Offray. Where the colour of a ribbon is described with a capital initial letter (ie Apple Green), this is the name of the particular Offray shade used for the item illustrated.

BRODERIE ANGLAISE: In the United States this is known as eyelet embroidery.

HEMS: In some instances it is necessary to turn the raw edge under when making a hem, eg to form a channel to carry elastic. But a double hem can be bulky on small garments, so where possible it is usually better to turn the hem under only once, and then sew across it with a herring-bone-stitch to prevent fraying. In such cases, it is helpful if you are able to cut your edge along the thread of the fabric.

ROSES: It is, of course, possible to buy various kinds of artificial flowers, and some of these appear in the book. But in many instances the outfits, and also the furniture, are trimmed with roses made from satin ribbon. These are easy to make and very economical, especially when compared with purchased artificial flowers. The width of the ribbon determines the size of the rose; and the longer it is, the more petals you will have. Miniature roses made from 3mm (⅛in) wide ribbon are especially pretty: but they are a bit fiddly, so it's a good idea to practise on a slightly wider ribbon until you have mastered the art. You will find detailed instructions for making ribbon roses below.

BRAID TRIMMINGS: Look for silky dress and lampshade braids. When a very narrow braid is required, you will sometimes find you can cut down the centre of a wider braid to make two very narrow lengths. This is often the case with lampshade or furnishing braids, which are made so that they can be folded over the edge of the item they are trimming.

PLAITED RIBBON BRAID: Very narrow braids are often hard to find in the shops, and it is usually even more difficult to match the shade you are looking for. It needs only a little patience to plait narrow ribbon to make very attractive satin braid in just the shade (or combination of colours) you want. Full directions for making plaited ribbon braid are given below.

GLUE: Use a clear, all-purpose adhesive where glue is required. UHU is a very good choice: it is quick to dry, and the long nozzle at the head of the tube makes it extremely easy to use.

DRY STICK ADHESIVE: When it is necessary to stick fabric to card, a dry stick glue is best. Some glue sticks are only recommended for paper, so make sure the one you choose lists fabric as well. UHU Stic is excellent.

LATEX ADHESIVE: When making the furniture, this is the easiest way to stick large pieces of corrugated cardboard or paper together, especially if you use one which comes in a pot with a built-in brush (like Copydex). Also, you may find that wallpaper paste will not adhere to corrugated cardboard if the surface has been treated with a damp-proof finish: in this case, a latex adhesive will do the job perfectly (make sure that your covering paper is thick enough to be opaque).

WALLPAPER PASTE: Any kind of paper paste will do, but wallpaper paste is very much cheaper. Polycell Regular is ideal. Don't make it too stiff, and don't worry if it soaks into your fabric: it will dry without leaving a mark. If wallpaper paste won't adhere to corrugated cardboard, use latex adhesive.

CUTTING OUT THE FURNITURE: Use a sharp craft knife with a fairly thin blade. The OLFA is especially good because you can keep snapping off the tip of the blade as it becomes blunted. Always use a metal rule to cut out the pieces (never use a plastic or wooden ruler because your knife will cut into it). A table knife and ruler are the best tools for scoring card or board (areas to be scored are indicated by a broken line on the pattern or diagram).

ARROWS (ON CORRUGATED CARDBOARD): Arrows indicate the direction of the ridges. When there are no arrows, it doesn't matter.

MEASUREMENTS: Use either metric or imperial measurements, but *don't* compare the two because they may not be the same. Each design has been worked out individually to make it as simple as possible to follow: and to avoid the eye-strain of counting tiny fractions or milli-metres, the most practical measurement is always given. As long as you use one set of measurements only, and don't alternate between the two, you can be sure the result will be perfectly in proportion. When the direction of measurements is not specifically stated, the depth is usually given first, followed by the width: ie 10×20cm (4×8in) = 10cm (4in) deep × 20cm (8in) wide.

MATERIALS: You will find a list of recommended stockists and suppliers (including mail order) at the end of the book (chapter 15), but most of the items used are very widely available.

RIBBON BOWS

You can, of course, just tie a bow in a piece of ribbon. But in most cases the result will be far more attractive if you take a little trouble and make your bow in one of the following ways. The first is very effective when you are using a wide ribbon: it looks wonderful at the back of a broad sash. The second version is a quick method which works very well with narrower ribbons, and makes a very attractive trimming for bodices, skirts and sleeves. (It's also perfect for William's top-knot!)

METHOD A

1. Fold under the cut ends of your piece of ribbon (the directions will tell you how long it should be), so that they overlap at the centre back (figure a).

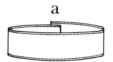

2. Gather the centre (figure b) and draw up, binding tightly several times with your thread to hold it securely (figure c).

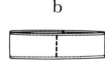

3. Fold a scrap of ribbon lengthways into three and bind it closely round the centre: secure the ends at the back and trim off the surplus neatly (figure d).

4. Gather across the centre of another piece of ribbon (length again as specified), then draw up tightly and fold it round, as figure e, for the ties.

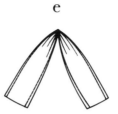

5. Stitch the ties behind the bow and trim the cut ends in an inverted V-shape (figure f).

METHOD B

1. Hold your piece of ribbon (the directions will tell you how long it should be) and curve it round as figure a. Pin it to hold.

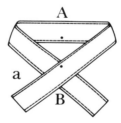

2. Using matching thread, take your needle through the ribbon at the dot below A (from behind, so the point comes towards you): then bring it through the two front ends where they cross, at the dot above B.

3. Draw up and then bind your thread tightly round and round the centre of the bow several times, finishing off neatly at the back (figure b): you may find it helps to gather between A-B first.

4. Trim the cut ends in an inverted V-shape.

PLAITED BRAID

Very narrow braids are necessary if the trimming is to be in proportion with the dainty Kate Greenaway clothes. It is also essential to give the furniture that elegant finishing touch. But narrow braids are often hard to find in the shops, especially if you are trying to match a particular shade. It is very easy to make your own satin braid by plaiting Offray 1.5mm (1/16in) wide ribbon; and the colour range is so comprehensive that you can nearly always find just the matching, toning or contrasting shade you require. Even more exciting: you can plait two or three different shades together, to make a multi-coloured, custom-designed braid to tone with a plain or patterned fabric.

1. The directions for the item you are making will usually tell you how much ribbon you need to make the length of braid you require. For instance: 'make a plait from three 25cm (10in) lengths of 1.5mm (1/16in) ribbon'. In this case, if you are making the braid in one colour only, cut one 25cm (10in) length of ribbon, and one 50cm (20in) length. Fold the longer piece in half, smear a trace of glue inside the fold, place one end of the shorter piece between the fold, then pinch together (figure a).

Fold

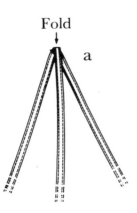

a

2. Push a pin through the folded end and secure it to a drawing board or something similar. Then begin to plait very evenly, making sure the strands of ribbon are always flat – never fold them over. Keep the ribbon taut, and draw the plait very firmly between your fingertips every 2–3cm (inch or so) to make it smooth and even (figure b). Hold the ends together with a paper clip.

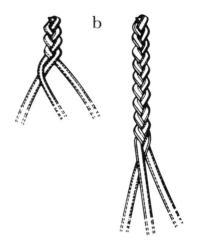

b

3. Glue the braid into place, spreading the glue just beyond the point where you intend cutting it, to ensure it does not unravel: press the cut ends down well, adding a little more glue if necessary.

4. Where actual lengths are not given in the directions, calculate the amount needed as follows: measure the length of braid you require and add a third. For example: if you need a 30cm (12in) length of braid, plait three pieces of ribbon 40cm (16in) long. If you want to make a multi-colour braid in two or three toning shades, divide the total amount by three to calculate the quantity of each ribbon you will require.

SATIN ROSES

You can make roses in all shapes and sizes from satin ribbon. The wider the ribbon, the bigger your rose: the longer the ribbon, the more petals it will have. The directions will tell you the width and length to use for each design, but you will soon be able to judge this for yourself. Use single-face satin ribbon (except for miniature 3mm (⅛in) roses) and matching thread.

1. Cut a length of ribbon as directed. Fold the corner as the broken line on figure a and bring point A down to meet point B as figure b. Fold again as the broken line on figure b and bring point C over A to meet point B as figure c. (Omit the second fold for 3mm ribbon.)

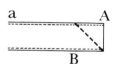

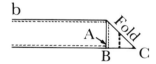

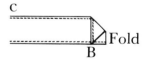

2. Now roll the ribbon round about four turns, with the folded corner inside, to form a tight tube, and make a few stitches through the base to hold (figure d). This forms the centre of the rose.

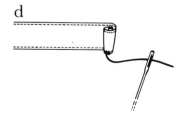

3. To make the petals, fold the ribbon down so the edge is aligned with the tube (figure e). Then curve the ribbon round the tube to form a cone, keeping the top of the tube level with the diagonal fold. When the tube again lies parallel to the remaining ribbon, make two or three stitches at the base to hold the petal you have just made (figure f).

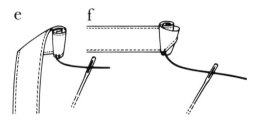

4. Continue to make petals with the remainder of the ribbon, sewing each one to the base of the flower before starting the next (figure g). Shape the rose as you work by gradually making the petals a little more open.

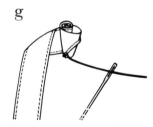

5. Finish the cut end neatly underneath the base of the completed rose (figure h).

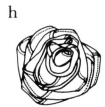

IF THIS IS YOUR VERY FIRST DOLL

For anyone who has never made a doll before, the Kate Greenaway doll is the ideal way to begin. Study the list of materials to see what you will need. So-called 'flesh-coloured' felt can sometimes be much too florid: if the colour is too strong, look for a deep cream or *very* pale pink. If you want to make a dark-skinned doll with black hair, choose a mid-brown felt (the colour of coffee with just a little cream stirred in!).

Read the Guidelines above on *tracing patterns* and prepare the ones for the basic doll as explained in chapter 3: cut separate patterns for the head back and front, and the body back and front. Pull the felt in both directions before you pin on the patterns: you will probably find that one way has more 'give' than the other. It is important to pin the pattern pieces for the arms and legs in this direction, so that when you stuff them they will stretch from top to bottom, and not across. The worst thing you can do is to cut one arm or leg *along* the direction of the 'stretch', and the second one *across* it: this will give you one long, thin arm or leg and one short and fat!

Careful cutting out is really very important because it determines the shape of your finished doll. It also makes it much easier to stitch the pieces together. One is always so anxious to start sewing that it is tempting to hurry through this stage, but do take your time and follow the edge of the pattern very accurately, cutting just a fraction outside it, so that you don't damage it. Use a soft pencil to transfer all the markings to the wrong side of your felt. (Felt doesn't have a 'right side' and a 'wrong side': so as soon as you have transferred your markings – *that* will be the wrong side.)

Follow the directions for making the doll (chapter 3) in the correct order: if you don't, you may find yourself in trouble! Pin the pieces, right sides

together, and oversew very neatly with small stitches, quite close together.

The stumbling block for most inexperienced doll-makers is the stuffing. If a doll isn't stuffed properly, it will never look right. But as long as you follow the rules, there is no reason why your very first doll shouldn't be perfect. A good stuffing is essential: don't use one which is lumpy, and don't use foam chips. A top-quality washable polyester is the best choice, but kapok is equally good (though it might make you sneeze!).

The great secret of successful stuffing is *patience*. Use a little stuffing at a time, teased out so that you are not feeding in solid lumps: then push it well down before inserting the next piece. As each area begins to fill up, mould it from the outside with your hands, smoothing and squeezing and rolling it into shape: make the head smooth and round – with special emphasis on the face. Always stuff very firmly, unless the instructions tell you otherwise. An understuffed doll can be a disaster because she will tend to get flatter and floppier the more she is cuddled – and who wants a doll that hangs her head in shame! If her neck doesn't hold up too firmly, insert a thin stick (as described in chapter 3). When you think you have stuffed the body sufficiently, sew on the legs as instructed; but just before you finish, add a bit *more* stuffing to round out her seat nicely. Sew the arms on very securely (make all your stitches in the same place to allow freedom of movement), and joint the elbows and knees so that she can move naturally.

Now all you have to do is choose a hairstyle and follow the directions for applying the yarn; then bring your doll to life with her features. See the Guidelines for cutting the eyes, and make sure the position is right before you glue them on.

And that's all there is to it. You have made your very first doll. Your only problem now is deciding which outfit to make first. Think about it while you're sewing her chemise and pantalettes!

CHAPTER 3

THE KATE GREENAWAY DOLL

How to make the basic doll

Use a firm, flesh-coloured felt and check that the quality is good. Buy it either by the metre (yard) or in squares, but make sure you cut all the pieces with the grain running in the same direction: there is a certain amount of stretch in felt, and this will become evident when the doll is stuffed. For greatest accuracy, and ease of cutting, trace the leg onto folded paper and open it out to cut the felt flat. Always oversew the edges to join.

– MATERIALS –

20cm (8in) flesh-coloured felt, 90cm (36in) wide
OR four 20cm (8in) squares
OR three 23cm (9in) squares
OR two 30cm (12in) squares
Scrap of mid-brown, olive green or blue felt for the eyes
Polyester stuffing
One ball (30–40g or 1–1½oz) thick knitting yarn for the hair
Stranded red embroidery cotton
2 domed black sequins, 8mm (⁵⁄₁₆in) diameter (or use black felt)
Matching and black sewing threads
Thin stick, 15cm (6in) long (optional)
Scrap of stiff card
Clear adhesive

———— · ————

1. Cut the head front and back, and the body front and back, once each. Cut the arm four times, and the leg and sole twice each. (If using 23cm (9in) squares,

cut the two heads and bodies and soles out of one: cut one leg and two arms out of each of the other two.) Mark the notches carefully. Cut the sole twice more in stiff card, but slightly smaller, as indicated on the pattern by the broken line.

2. Gather across the lower edge of the front head, between crosses: pin to the top edge of the body front, draw up to fit, then oversew the head and neck together. Join the back head to the body back in the same way.

3. Gather close to the edge of the front head, between the circles. Pin the head pieces together, matching crosses and notches. Draw up the gathers to fit, distributing them evenly between the notches, then join all round, leaving the straight neck edge open between crosses.

4. Join the side edges of the body, below crosses, stitching especially securely around the neck. Turn to the right side.

5. Stuff the head very firmly, working slowly and carefully, moulding it into a smoothly rounded shape. If the neck tends to wobble, stiffen it by pushing a thin stick up the centre of the body and into the head, then complete stuffing the neck and body round it.

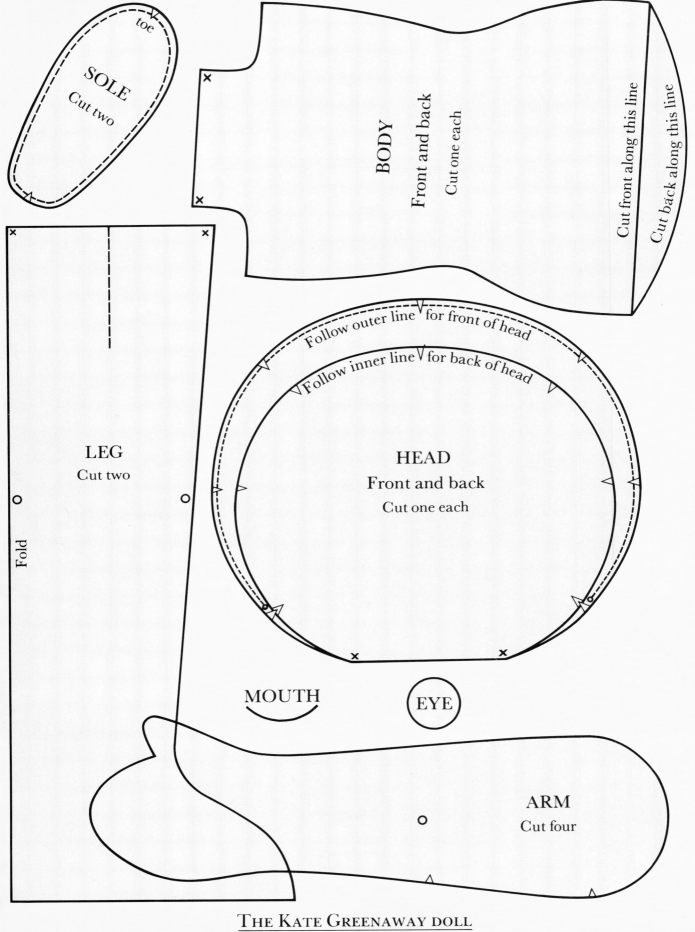

THE KATE GREENAWAY DOLL

6. Join two pieces for each arm, leaving open between the notches: make tiny stitches, close together, around the hand and thumb. Turn to the right side, stuff firmly and close the seam.

7. Fold each leg in half, as pattern, and join the centre front seam between the top and toe. Fit the sole inside the lower edge, matching notches to front seam (toe) and centre back of leg: oversew together. Turn to the right side. Fit the card sole inside and hold in place temporarily with pins from the outside (push through the felt into the cut edge of the card). Stuff the leg firmly, then pin the top edges together, *matching crosses so centre front seam meets centre back of leg*, folding at each side as indicated by the broken line. Gather across the top and draw up to measure 3cm (1¼in).

8. Pin the legs, side by side and toes forward, to the inside of the body front (check the feet are level): stitch securely. Pin the lower edge of the body back over the legs, level with the front stitching line. Join across one leg, then complete stuffing the body before sewing the other leg.

9. Sew the tops of the arms securely to the shoulders to allow free movement in all directions.

10. Make elbow and knee joints at the circles. Working from the outside, ease the stuffing up and down the limb, away from the circles, by bending the limb backwards and forwards: using double thread, make tiny stitches through the limb between the circles, pulling very tight. 'Work' the elbows and knees again to make them bend easily.

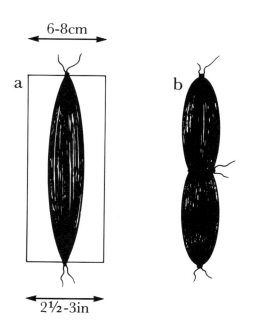

HAIRSTYLES

All the hairstyles are made by stitching small 'skeins' of yarn over the head. To make a skein, cut a piece of stiff card 6–8cm (2½–3in) wide by the depth required. Wrap the yarn evenly round the card ten times (more if the yarn is thinner): tie the loops tightly at each edge with a single strand of yarn (figure a). Slip the skein off the card and tie the centre a little more loosely (figure b). Using matching thread (and a long darning needle), stitch the centre of the skein to the head as directed: when you have done this, spread a little glue underneath before fixing the ends to hold the section in place at each side. Trim off the centre ties and loose ends of yarn neatly.

– LOUISA –

1st skein: 23cm (9in) deep. Stitch the centre to the centre top of the head, over the seam. Take the sides smoothly down over the seam and stitch the ends at the base.

2nd skein: 22cm (8⅝in) deep. Stitch centre to front of head, close to the first skein. Take the sides smoothly down (pulling quite tight) and stitch the ends *over* the previous ones.

3rd skein: 13cm (5¼in) deep. Stitch the centre and ends to the back of the head, immediately behind the 1st skein.

4th skein: 11.5cm (4½in) deep. Stitch immediately behind the 3rd skein.

5th skein: 10cm (4in) deep. Stitch immediately behind the 4th skein.

6th skein: 8.5cm (3⅜in) deep. Stitch immediately behind the 5th skein.

7th skein: 7cm (2¾in) deep. Stitch immediately behind the 6th skein to finish at the nape of the neck. (If the head is not fully covered, add one or more skeins, of the length required, before completing with the final one.)

Make seven clusters of curls by winding the yarn ten times round a 4cm (1½in) deep piece of card. Slide off carefully and bind the centre tightly with matching thread, then fold over and stitch securely to form a bunch of loops. Stitch one at the centre top point of the forehead, with two more, side by side, just below: then stitch one at each side, just below the previous two. Stitch the remaining bunches at each side of the head immediately in front of the ends of the 1st and 2nd skeins.

– EMILY –

1st and 2nd skeins: As for Louisa, but don't glue the 2nd skein. Instead, when it is fixed, draw the 2nd skein back towards the 1st with a thread around both skeins, catching them to the head at points 3cm (1¼in) each side of the centre (so that the hair is caught up at each side of the forehead).

Next skein: 6cm (2½in) deep. Stitch the centre to the head, in front of the 2nd skein. Take each end smoothly across the forehead to form the hairline, and stitch inside the angle formed by the previous step.

Complete the back of the head as for Louisa, beginning at '3rd skein'.

Make about twelve curls by winding the yarn *tightly* ten times round the tip of your forefinger. Catch the loops securely together at one side, then stitch to the head: three in the angle at each side of the forehead, with two underneath, one below the other. Stitch one more curl at each side of the face, just in front of the ends of the 2nd skein. Add more curls over the temples, if necessary.

– CHARLOTTE –

Initial skein: This is a little different from the rest. Wind the yarn *twenty* times around a 17cm (6¾in) deep card. Tie the loops at the bottom edge *quite loosely*, then *cut* the loops at the top edge. Carefully remove the card and tie the centre *very loosely*. Place the skein over the head, across the top seam, with the cut ends over the forehead and the other half of the skein covering the back of the head, the tied loops at the nape of the neck: catch these securely across the back of the head about 4–5mm (³⁄₁₆in) above the neck seam. Move the centre tie to correspond with the seam, and catch the hair to the top of the head.

Next two skeins: As the 1st and 2nd skeins for Louisa.

4th skein: 20cm (8in) deep. Stitch the centre to the back of the head immediately behind the 2nd skein: take each side smoothly down to fill in the back of the head. Stitch the ends level with the ends of the previous skeins. (If this is insufficient to cover the head, add another skein or make the 4th skein a little thicker.)

Bun: Wind the yarn *fifteen* times around the 17cm (6¾in) card. Tie the ends, but *not* the centre. Remove and make a loose knot at the middle of the skein, then knot together the end ties and tuck them underneath the bun. Stitch to the crown of the head.

Make two curls, as for Emily, and stitch one at each side of the head, over the ends of the 2nd and 3rd skeins.

– MARY-ANNE –

Follow the directions for Charlotte from the initial skein up to (but not including) the bun. Make seven clusters of curls as directed for Louisa. Stitch one at the centre top, just in front of the 2nd skein and over the fringe. Draw the 2nd skein back at each side of the fringe, 3cm (1¼in) from the centre (as Emily), and stitch a bunch in this position. Stitch another bunch at each side, over the fringe, between the first two, and then another at each side of the face, below the others. Finally, make two curls as for Emily, and stitch them below the last two bunches.

Make five more clusters of curls. Stitch one at each side of the head, over the ends of the 2nd and 3rd skeins, then stitch the remaining three across the back of the head, over the ends of the skeins.

FEATURES

1. Cut the eye twice in felt. Stitch a sequin in the centre of each (or cut small felt circles and glue them to the eye using tweezers). Pin the eyes to the face to determine their position. If you don't trust yourself to do this 'by eye', push a pin into the centre of the face, about 4.5cm (1¾in) above the neck seam (be guided a little by your hairstyle). Position the eyes each side of this pin, with a 2.5cm (1in) space between them.

2. Using black thread, make two or three tiny 3mm (⅛in) straight stitches, in the same place, for the nose. The nose should be level with the bottom of the eyes.

3. Embroider the mouth in stem (outline) stitch, using three strands of embroidery cotton, about 1cm (⅜in) below the nose.

4. Glue the eyes in place.

CHAPTER 4

UP WITH THE LARK

*S*leepy Louisa is having such a lovely dream that she doesn't want to get up. But it's her birthday, and everyone has flowers for her, so Charlotte is ready with some encouragement from above.

Any light- to medium-weight fabric is suitable for the girls' dainty lingerie, but avoid fabric which is loosely woven and might fray. All of the under pinnings illustrated are made from spotted voile, which is ideal for the purpose as well as being very feminine. But a cotton-type fabric in white or in a plain pastel shade, or with a tiny floral print, would be equally attractive. Try to match the colour and/or trimmings to the dress which is to be worn on top.

Emily (standing), Charlotte and Louisa all wear full-length chemises over their pantalettes. But Mary-Anne (playing with the dog) has a separate camisole and petticoat.

EMILY'S CHEMISE AND PANTALETTES

– MATERIALS –

25cm (10in) white spotted voile, 75cm (30in) wide
20cm (8in) broderie anglaise, 25mm (1in) deep
20cm (8in) very narrow white lace, 7–8mm (¼in) deep
1.10m (1¼yd) white lace, 15–20mm (½–¾in) deep: select a design through which you can slot 1.5mm (¹⁄₁₆in) ribbon
1.10m (1¼yd) Light Orchid satin ribbon, 1.5mm (¹⁄₁₆in) wide
20cm (8in) Light Orchid satin ribbon, 3mm (⅛in) wide
10cm (4in) Grape satin ribbon, 3mm (⅛in) wide
20cm (8in) narrow round elastic
Shirring elastic
2 snap fasteners
Clear adhesive

– CHEMISE –

1. Cut the skirt pattern in voile. Mark notches along the top edge, then gather. Mark the broderie anglaise equally into eight. Right sides together and raw edges level, pin the top edge of the skirt to the broderie anglaise, matching notches to marked points: draw up the skirt to fit, and stitch, distributing gathers evenly. Turn raw edges up behind broderie anglaise and top-stitch neatly to hold in place.

2. Join the centre back edges of the skirt, leaving open at the top as indicated on the pattern. Turn in the raw edges of the skirt and broderie anglaise above the

Note: See also the Party-going illustration (page 74) for Louisa's chemise and pantalettes and Mary-Anne's petticoat.
Directions for Louisa's Nightgown and Nightcap are in chapter 11.
Directions for the Fairytale Four-poster Bed and Rosebud and Ribbons Bedroom Table are in chapter 13.

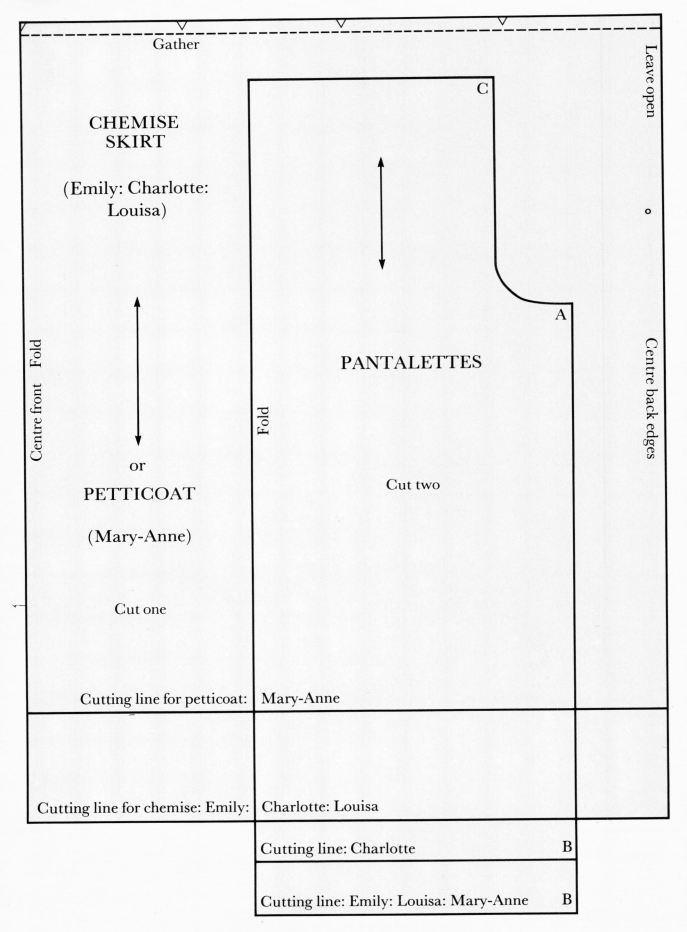

Gather

Leave open

CHEMISE
SKIRT

(Emily: Charlotte:
Louisa)

C

Centre front   Fold

Centre back edges

PANTALETTES

Fold

A

or
PETTICOAT

(Mary-Anne)

Cut two

Cut one

Cutting line for petticoat: Mary-Anne

Cutting line for chemise: Emily: Charlotte: Louisa

Cutting line: Charlotte   B

Cutting line: Emily: Louisa: Mary-Anne   B

FOUR SETS OF UNDERPINNINGS

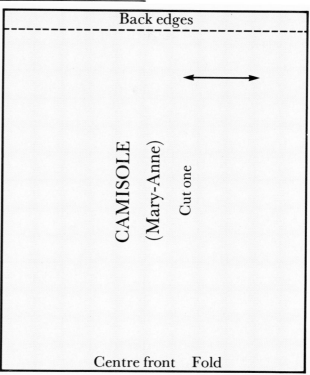

Left pattern (Chemise/Bodice):

Back | edges

Cut one

CHEMISE

BODICE

Fold | Centre front

Right pattern (Camisole):

Back edges

CAMISOLE
(Mary-Anne)

Cut one

Centre front   Fold

---

centre back seam, and make narrow hems. Fit on the doll to check overlap for centre back opening, then sew on two snap fasteners to close.

3. To make each shoulder strap, cut a 10cm (4in) length of very narrow lace. Cut a 13cm (5in) length of shirring elastic and fold it in half to use double. Stitch the elastic in and out through the lace, close to the straight edge: draw up the elastic, knot both ends, and stitch very securely to the lace. Fit the chemise on the doll and mark the position of the straps at front and back, then sew in place.

4. Glue the wider Light Orchid ribbon around the lower edge of the broderie anglaise for the waistband. Make a tiny ribbon rose from the deeper shade (see chapter 2), and stitch at centre front of band.

5. Turn up a 1cm (⅜in) hem around the lower edge. Slot narrow ribbon

through the top edge of the lace, then stitch lace around the lower edge of the skirt, overlapping about 1cm (⅜in). Stitch another row of ribbon-slotted lace 3cm (1¼in) above the first one.

– PANTALETTES –

6. Cut the pattern twice in voile (note longer cutting line).

7. Fold each piece in half and join the side seam A–B. Right sides together, join the two pieces between A and C for the centre front and back seams. Clip the curve and press the seams open.

8. Turn under the raw top edge and make a 1cm (⅜in) hem. Turn up a narrow hem around the lower edge of each leg. Turn to the right side.

9. Thread round elastic through the waist hem and draw up to fit the doll.

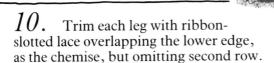

10. Trim each leg with ribbon-slotted lace overlapping the lower edge, as the chemise, but omitting second row.

CHARLOTTE'S CHEMISE AND PANTALETTES

– MATERIALS –

30cm (12in) cream spotted voile, 75cm (30in) wide
20cm (8in) very narrow blue lace, 7–8mm (¼in) deep
1.60m (1¾yd) blue lace, 10mm (⅜in) deep
20cm (8in) blue ribbon, 3mm (⅛in) wide (to match lace)
10cm (4in) Rosy Mauve satin ribbon, 3mm (⅛in) wide
50cm (½yd) narrow round elastic
Shirring elastic
2 snap fasteners
Clear adhesive

———— · ————

– CHEMISE –

1. Cut the skirt and bodice patterns once each in voile. Mark the notches. Right sides together and raw edges level, pin the top edge of the skirt to the bodice, matching notches: draw up the skirt to fit, then stitch, distributing the gathers evenly. Turn under a small hem along each side edge of the bodice and tack. Fold the bodice over, wrong side inside, as broken line: turn the raw lower edge under and slip-stitch over the skirt gathers. Slip-stitch side edges of bodice neatly. Top-stitch the bodice just above the waist join.

2. Join the centre back edges of the skirt, leaving open at the top as indicated on pattern. Turn in the raw edges above the centre back seam and make narrow hems. Fit on the doll to check overlap for centre back opening, then sew on two snap fasteners to close.

3. Follow step 3 (shoulder straps) for Emily's Chemise (above).

4. Stitch wider blue lace around the top edge of the bodice. Glue blue ribbon around the lower edge of the bodice for the waistband. Make a tiny Rosy Mauve ribbon rose (see chapter 2), and stitch at centre front of band.

5. Turn up a 1cm (⅜in) hem around the lower edge. Stitch lace along the edge, overlapping below. Then stitch a second band just above.

– PANTALETTES –

6. Cut the pattern twice in voile (note shorter cutting line).

7. Follow steps 7, 8 and 9 for Emily's Pantalettes (above), but make a double hem around the lower edge of each leg.

8. Trim each leg with two bands of lace, as the chemise. Thread elastic through hems and draw up to fit ankles.

LOUISA'S CHEMISE AND PANTALETTES

– MATERIALS –

30cm (12in) white spotted voile, 75cm (30in) wide
·2.10m (2¼yd) very narrow white lace, 7–8mm (¼in) deep
40cm (16in) very narrow pink and green embroidered flower trimming
30cm (12in) pink satin ribbon, 1.5mm (¹⁄₁₆in) wide
20cm (8in) narrow round elastic
Shirring elastic
2 snap fasteners

———— · ————

– CHEMISE –

1. Follow steps 1 and 2 for Charlotte's Chemise (above), *but note the longer cutting line for the skirt.*

2. Follow step 3 (shoulder straps) for Emily's Chemise (above).

3. Stitch embroidered trimming around the top edge of the bodice. Fold ribbon in half and sew at centre of lower edge of bodice, then stitch trimming around the lower edge, over the ribbon.

4. Stitch one row of lace overlapping the lower edge of the hem, with two more above, 2–3mm (⅛in) apart.

– PANTALETTES –

5. Cut the pattern twice in voile (note longer cutting line).

6. Follow steps 7, 8 and 9 for Emily's Pantalettes (above).

7. Trim each leg with two rows of lace, about 5mm (¼in) apart.

NB Louisa's chemise and pantalettes can be seen in chapter 10.

MARY-ANNE'S CAMISOLE, PETTICOAT AND PANTALETTES

– MATERIALS –

30cm (12in) white spotted voile, 75cm (30in) wide
20cm (8in) very narrow coffee lace, 7–8mm (¼in) deep
2m (2¼yd) coffee lace, 10mm (⅜in) deep
20cm (8in) Sable brown satin ribbon, 1.5mm (¹⁄₁₆in) wide
30cm (12in) Sable brown satin ribbon, 3mm (⅛in) wide
35cm (14in) white bias binding
75cm (30in) narrow round elastic
Shirring elastic
2 snap fasteners

——————— · ———————

– CAMISOLE –

1. Cut the pattern in voile. Turn the raw edge under and then turn over and stitch a very narrow hem along the top and bottom edges. Make similar hems, but 5mm (¼in) wide (as broken line), down both sides.

2. Fit on the doll to check overlap for centre back, then sew on snap fasteners at top and halfway down.

3. Follow step 3 (shoulder straps) for Emily's Chemise (above).

4. Mark the centre front, then stitch two vertical rows of lace so the straight edges overlap along the centre line. Stitch one row of lace along the top edge, overlapping about 4–5mm (³⁄₁₆in), with another row overlapping the lower edge of the first one.

5. Make a tiny rose from 3mm (⅛in) ribbon (as chapter 2) and stitch at the centre front.

6. Make three tiny bows from 6cm (2½in) lengths of 1.5mm (¹⁄₁₆in) ribbon (method B in chapter 2) and stitch down the centre front, below the rose.

– PETTICOAT –

7. Cut the pattern in voile (note the shorter cutting line). Join the centre back edges.

8. Turn under the raw top edge and make a 1cm (⅜in) hem. Thread round elastic through the hem and draw up to fit the doll.

9. Turn up a 1cm (⅜in) hem around the lower edge. Turn to the right side.

10. Stitch a band of lace so that it almost completely overlaps the lower edge: stitch two more rows above, 2–3mm (⅛in) apart. Make a bow from a 6cm (2½in) length of 3mm (⅛in) ribbon (method B in chapter 2) and stitch at centre front, over the top row of lace.

NB Mary-Anne's petticoat can be seen in chapter 10.

— PANTALETTES —

11. Cut the pattern twice in voile (note longer cutting line).

12. Follow step 7 for Emily's Pantalettes (above).

13. Turn under the raw top edge and make a 1cm (⅜in) hem. Turn up a narrow hem around the lower edge of each leg. Stitch bias binding to form a channel round each ankle, 1.5cm (½in) above the lower edge.

14. Turn to the right side and trim each leg with three rows of lace, as the petticoat (step 10). Make two more bows and stitch one at each side, over the top row of lace.

15. Thread round elastic through the waist and ankles, and draw up to fit the doll.

SHOES, PUMPS AND SLIPPERS

*Y*ou can vary the basic pattern in all kinds of ways, as you will see from the illustrations. Black pumps can be plain or tied with long strings: coloured slippers can be matched to a special outfit and trimmed with roses, bows and frilly lace.

— MATERIALS —

14cm (5½in) square of black felt
OR 10cm (4in) square of coloured and an 8cm (3in) square of brown felt
1m (1yd) black satin ribbon, 1.5mm (¹⁄₁₆in) wide for ties (optional)
20cm (8in) satin ribbon, 3mm (⅛in) wide for roses (optional)
Clear adhesive if adding rose trim (optional)

———— · ————

1. Cut the upper four times and the sole twice (for coloured shoes, cut the soles in brown).

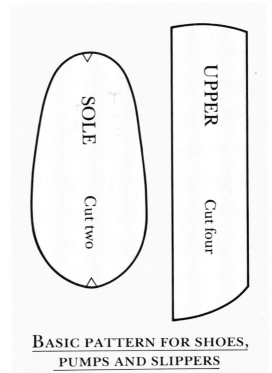

BASIC PATTERN FOR SHOES, PUMPS AND SLIPPERS

2. For each shoe join two uppers, oversewing at the front and back. Pin the lower edge to the sole, matching seams to notches, then oversew. Turn to the right side.

3. For the ties, cut very narrow ribbon in two 50cm (½yd) lengths and stitch the centre inside the shoe, at the top of the back seam. Criss-cross around the leg and tie at the back, as illustrated.

4. Make two tiny roses (see chapter 2) from 10cm (4in) ribbon each – for a larger rose, use up to 15cm (6in) ribbon – and glue or sew to the front of the shoe. The slippers waiting beside Louisa's bed have lace rosettes made from 10cm (4in) of 10mm (⅜in) deep lace: overlap and join (sew or glue) the cut ends to form a circle, then gather the straight edge and draw up to leave a tiny hole – about 3mm (⅛in) diameter – in the centre. Stitch to the shoe, then glue a rose in the centre.

CHAPTER 5

BIRTHDAY BREAKFAST

*E*veryone *(including William) is joining in the excitement as Louisa opens her birthday cards and presents. She's thrilled with her beautiful new doll, and can't wait to begin making lots more pretty clothes for it (see overleaf).*

The girls (left to right, Louisa, Emily, Mary-Anne and Charlotte) are all wearing simple day dresses attractively trimmed with lace, braid and ribbon. Mob caps are essential in the Greenaway household, and a pinafore or apron is often a good idea too, when you lead such a busy life!

CHARLOTTE'S DARK FLOWERED DRESS

*H*er favourite warm frock is made in a firmly woven printed fabric. Violet and blue cottage garden flowers are scattered over a black background, and the dress is trimmed with black lace. Underneath, Charlotte wears her cream undies which give a wicked peep of dainty blue lace beneath the skirt (pattern on page 34).

– MATERIALS –

25cm (¼yd) printed cotton-type fabric, 90cm (36in) wide
90cm (1yd) black lace, 10–15mm (½in) deep
50cm (½yd) black bias binding
25cm (¼yd) narrow round elastic (preferably black)
2 snap fasteners

---·---

Note: Directions for William the Dog are in chapter 12.
Directions for the Breakfast Table and Stools are in chapter 13.

1. Cut the bodice front once and the back and sleeve twice each. Cut a piece 23cm (9in) deep × 40cm (16in) wide for the skirt.

2. Join the bodice front to the back pieces at each shoulder.

3. Mark the centre at the top edge of the sleeve, then gather between the circles. Fit the sleeve into the armhole of the bodice, matching side edges and notches, and centre top with the shoulder seam. Draw up the gathers to fit, distributing them evenly between the marked points, and stitch. Clip curves. When both sleeves are in place, join the side seams of the sleeves and bodice.

4. Bind the wrist edge of each sleeve, folding the binding over the raw edge. Stitch lace just above the binding, to overlap the edge of the sleeve. Thread 11cm (4¼in) elastic through the binding and draw up to fit the doll.

5. Mark the top edge of the skirt equally into eight, then gather, beginning and ending 2cm (¾in) from the side edges. Pin to the lower edge of the bodice, matching marked points to notches and seams. Draw up to fit, and stitch, distributing the gathers evenly. Turn the gathers up inside and top-stitch close to the lower edge of the bodice. Join the centre back seam of the skirt, leaving 5cm (2in) open at the top. Turn under the centre back edges of the bodice as broken line and stitch: turn under and stitch the edges of the skirt opening to correspond.

6. Bind the neck edge, then stitch lace on top to form a tiny stand-up collar.

7. Stitch snap fasteners to the back opening at neck and waist.

8. Fit the dress on the doll and turn up the hem, then stitch lace on top, as illustrated.

CHARLOTTE'S SPOTTED VOILE PINAFORE

This sensible pinafore is practical but pretty with a yoke of ruffled broderie anglaise, and a hem trimmed with narrow lace. White or cream are the most appropriate colours: Charlotte's is cream spotted voile to match her chemise and pantalettes (pattern on page 35).

– MATERIALS –

22×40cm (9×16in) cream spotted voile (or similar fabric)
40cm (½yd) cream broderie anglaise, 30mm (1¼in) deep
45cm (½yd) narrow cream lace, about 10mm (⅜in) deep
1.30m (1½yd) cream bias binding
Snap fastener

———— · ————

1. Cut the pattern piece in folded fabric.

2. Bind the hem, then bind the straight back edges. Bind each armhole, then overlap and stitch the ends of the armhole bindings to form shoulder joins.

3. Mark the broderie anglaise equally into four: gather, then pin around the neck edge, matching the marked points at centre front and shoulders. Draw up the gathers evenly to fit, and stitch. Bind the raw edges neatly.

4. Stitch lace around the hem, and stitch snap fastener at the top of the back opening.

CHARLOTTE'S MATCHING MOB CAP

To complete her demure daytime cover-up, tuck her curls into an easy-to-make mob cap, finished with a big satin bow to match her dress.

– MATERIALS –

Two 30cm (12in) diameter circles of cream spotted voile (or similar fabric as pinafore)
30cm (12in) narrow round elastic
25cm (10in) single-face satin ribbon, 16mm (⅝in) wide

———— · ————

1. To draw your pattern, fold a sheet of tracing paper – at least 35cm (13in) square – into four. Place folds against lines as indicated, matching the corner carefully. Trace (line A) and cut out through the four thicknesses. Open out and cut in double fabric.

2. Right sides together, join the two circles all round the outside, leaving 8cm (3in) open for turning. Using pinking shears, trim the edge close to the seam. Turn in and tack the edge at each side of the opening. Turn to the right side and slip-stitch the edges of the opening. Make a row of tiny stitches, very close to the edge, to give a flat, crisp finish.

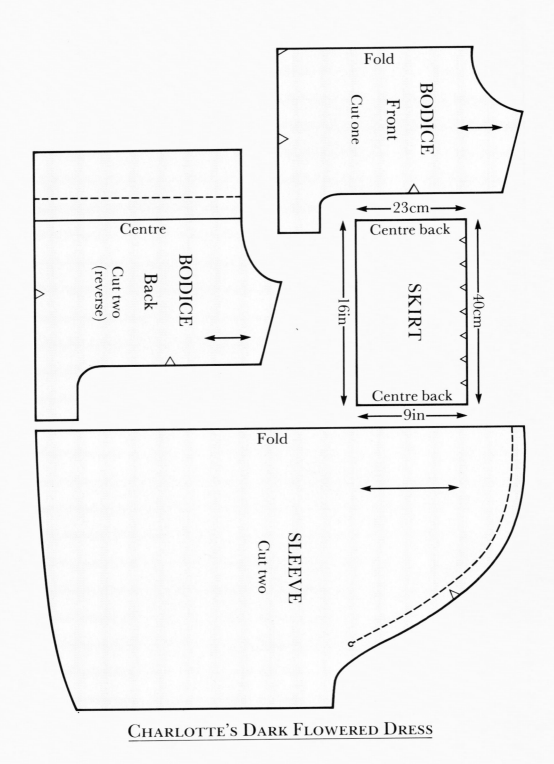

Fold

BODICE
Front
Cut one

BODICE
Back
Cut two
(reverse)

Centre

23cm

Centre back

SKIRT

16in

40cm

Centre back

9in

Fold

SLEEVE
Cut two

CHARLOTTE'S DARK FLOWERED DRESS

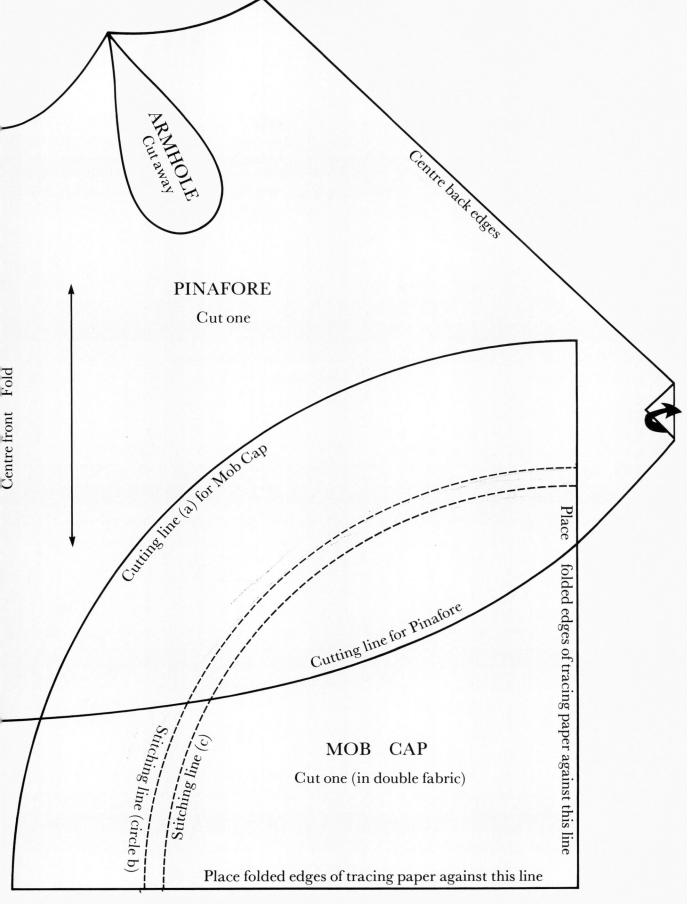

ARMHOLE
Cut away

Centre back edges

PINAFORE

Cut one

Centre front   Fold

Cutting line (a) for Mob Cap

Place

Cutting line for Pinafore

folded edges of tracing paper against this line

Stitching line (c)

Stitching line (circle b)

MOB   CAP

Cut one (in double fabric)

Place folded edges of tracing paper against this line

CHARLOTTE'S SPOTTED VOILE PINAFORE AND MATCHING
MOB CAP

3. Cut a circle of paper as the first pattern, but following line B on pattern: pin exactly in the centre of the cap. Stitch the fabric just beyond the edge of the paper: then remove it and make another circle of stitches about 5mm (¼in) inside the previous one (as line C on pattern). Press well, then thread elastic through the channel and draw up to fit the doll's head.

4. Make a bow (as method A in chapter 2) from a 12cm (5in) length of ribbon bound with a piece 3cm (1¼in) long: use the remainder to make the ties. Stitch at centre front of cap and trim the cut ends to length in an inverted V-shape.

LOUISA'S ALMOND GREEN BRAIDED DRESS

*L**ouisa chose a pale shade of green for this smart day dress because it goes so beautifully with her winter cloak (see chapter 9). Wrist length sleeves, a high neck and longer skirt mean that it's cosy at any time of the year, whilst cream lace combined with silky braid makes an unusual trimming.*

— MATERIALS —

25cm (¼yd) cotton-blend poplin (or similar fabric) 90cm (36in) wide
50cm (½yd) cream lace, 10mm (⅜in) deep
40cm (16in) cream lace, 25mm (1in) deep
10cm (4in) velvet ribbon, 15mm (⅝in) wide
50cm (½yd) narrow silky braid, 7mm (¼in) wide
50cm (½yd) matching bias binding
25cm (¼yd) narrow round elastic
2 snap fasteners

———— · ————

1. Cut the bodice front once and the back and sleeve twice each. Cut a piece 22cm (8¾in) deep × 40cm (16in) wide for the skirt.

2. Follow steps 2 and 3 for Charlotte's Dark Flowered Dress (above).

3. Bind the wrist edge of each sleeve, turning the full width of the binding over to the wrong side. Then stitch narrow lace to the right side of the sleeve, so the top edge of the lace covers 3–4mm (⅛in) of the fabric, and the rest overlaps the edge of the sleeve. Thread 11cm (4¼in) elastic through the binding (above the lace) and draw up to fit the doll's wrists.

4. Mark the top edge of the skirt equally into eight, then gather, beginning and ending 2cm (¾in) from the side edges. Pin to the lower edge of the bodice, matching the marked points to notches and seams. Draw up to fit, and stitch, distributing the gathers evenly. Turn the gathers up inside and top-stitch close to the lower edge of the bodice. Join the centre back seam of the skirt, leaving 5cm (2in) open at the top. Turn under the centre back edges of the bodice as broken line and stitch: turn under and stitch the edges of the skirt opening to correspond.

5. Bind the neck edge, then trim with narrow lace, stitching the straight edge of the lace to the folded top edge of the binding, to form a stand-up collar. Then stitch braid over the binding and the lower edge of the lace, finishing the ends neatly at the back.

6. Stitch snap fasteners to the back opening at neck and waist.

7. Catch velvet ribbon across the front of the bodice, for the waistband, turning the cut ends under at an angle to fit the armhole shaping.

8. Fit the dress on the doll and turn up the hem. Stitch wide lace around the hem as illustrated, followed by a band of braid over the top edge.

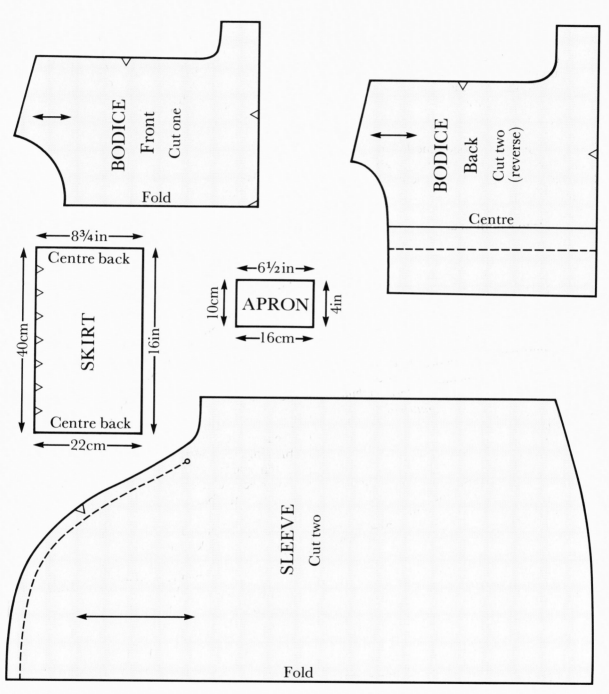

BODICE Front Cut one

Fold

BODICE Back Cut two (reverse)

Centre

8¾in
Centre back
SKIRT
40cm
16in
Centre back
22cm

6½in
10cm **APRON** 4in
16cm

SLEEVE Cut two

Fold

LOUISA'S ALMOND GREEN BRAIDED DRESS

LOUISA'S APRON AND MOB CAP

*V*ery pale blue contrasts prettily with her soft green dress. Louisa ties this little apron round her waist to protect her skirt when she is busy. And the matching cap, keeping her curls in place, is trimmed with the same velvet as her dress.

– MATERIALS –

35cm (14in) spotted voile (or similar fabric), 75cm (30in) wide
15cm (6in) velvet ribbon, 15mm (⅝in) wide
70cm (¾yd) satin ribbon (to match fabric), 3mm (⅛in) wide
30cm (12in) narrow round elastic

1. Cut a piece of fabric 16cm (6½in) deep × 10cm (4in) wide for the apron.

2. Turn under a narrow hem along the side and bottom edges.

3. Turn under the top edge also, but gather close to the fold: draw up to measure 6cm (2½in). Stitch satin ribbon behind the gathers, with the top edges of the ribbon and apron level and the centres matching so that the ends of the ribbon form ties.

4. Follow the directions for making Charlotte's Mob Cap (page 33), but make only the first part of the bow (omitting the ties) (step 4), using 12cm (5in) of velvet ribbon for the bow itself, and binding the centre with 3cm (1¼in).

MARY-ANNE'S LACE-TRIMMED BROWN DRESS

A versatile, basic style for any season, this typical Kate Greenaway frock can be trimmed in many attractive ways. The low neckline is very feminine – even more so when you add a softly draped shawl collar.

– MATERIALS –

25cm (¼yd) cotton-blend poplin (or similar fabric), 90cm (36in) wide
1.80m (2yd) coffee lace, 10mm (⅜in) deep
50cm (½yd) coffee or cream bias binding
2 snap fasteners

1. Cut the bodice front once and the back and sleeve twice each. Cut a piece 22cm (8¾in) deep × 40cm (16in) wide for the skirt.

2. Join the bodice front to the back pieces at each shoulder.

3. Mark the centre at the top edge of the sleeve, then gather between the circles. Fit the sleeve into the armhole of the bodice, matching side edges and notches, and centre top with shoulder seam. Draw up the gathers to fit, distributing them evenly between the marked points, and stitch. Clip curves. When both sleeves are in place, join the side seams of the sleeves and bodice.

4. Bind the wrist edge of each sleeve, folding the binding over the raw edge. Stitch lace over the binding to overlap the edge of the sleeve.

5. Mark the top edge of the skirt equally into eight, then gather, beginning and ending 2cm (¾in) from the side edges. Pin to the lower edge of the bodice, matching marked points to notches and seams. Draw up to fit and stitch, distributing the gathers evenly.

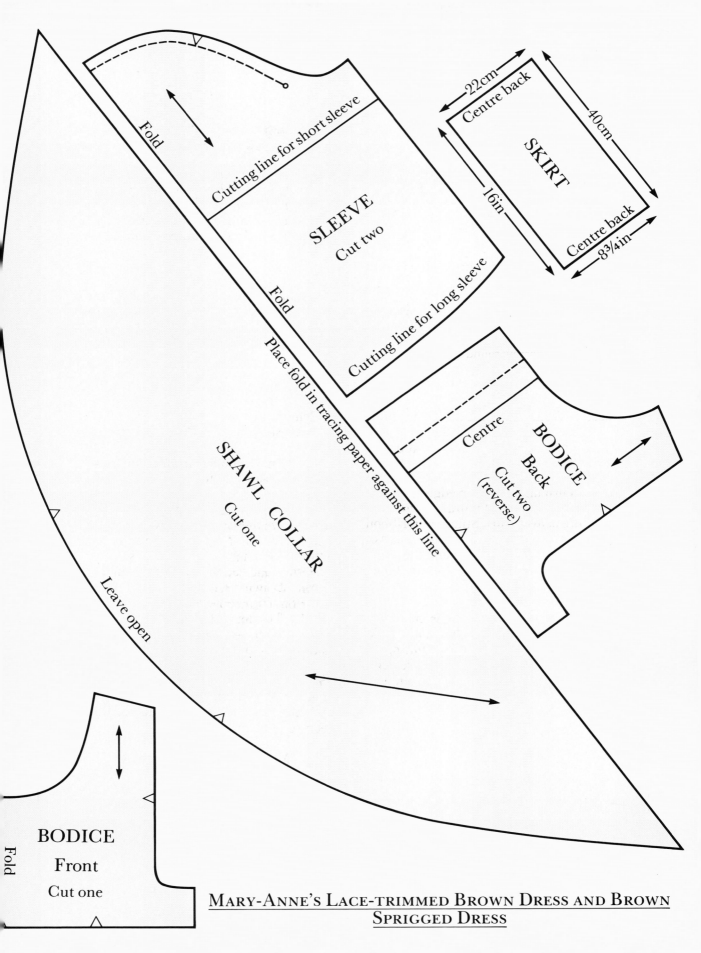

SLEEVE
Cut two

Cutting line for short sleeve

Cutting line for long sleeve

Fold

Fold

Place fold in tracing paper against this line

SHAWL COLLAR
Cut one

Leave open

SKIRT

22cm

40cm

16in

8¾in

Centre back

Centre back

BODICE
Back
Cut two
(reverse)

Centre

BODICE
Front
Cut one

Fold

MARY-ANNE'S LACE-TRIMMED BROWN DRESS AND BROWN
SPRIGGED DRESS

Turn the gathers up inside and top-stitch close to the lower edge of the bodice. Join the centre back seam of the skirt, leaving 5cm (2in) open at the top. Turn under the centre back edges of the bodice as broken line and stitch: turn under and stitch the edge of the skirt opening to correspond.

6. Bind the neck edge, then stitch slightly gathered lace on top.

7. Stitch snap fasteners to the back opening at neck and waist.

8. Fit the dress on the doll and turn up the hem, then stitch three rows of lace on top, 2–3mm (⅛in) apart, as illustrated.

MARY-ANNE'S SHAWL COLLAR AND MOB CAP

A soft, light-weight fabric is essential, so that the collar will drape gently round the neck. A very fine handkerchief lawn would do well or, as illustrated, a sheer lining silk, which Mary-Anne thinks is the perfect choice.

– MATERIALS –

35cm (14in) light-weight fabric, 90cm (36in) wide
50cm (½yd) coffee lace, 10mm (⅜in) deep
40cm (½yd) satin ribbon, 3mm (⅛in) wide
25cm (10in) single-face satin ribbon, 16mm (⅝in) wide
30cm (12in) narrow round elastic

———— · ————

1. Cut the collar pattern once (note direction of fabric – the collar is cut on the cross).

2. Fold diagonally (as pattern) right sides together and join the raw edges, leaving open at the centre, as indicated. Using pinking shears, trim the edge close to the seam and clip the corners. Turn in and tack the edge at each side of the

opening. Turn to the right side and slip-stitch the edges of the opening. Make a row of tiny stitches, very close to the seam, to give a flat, crisp finish.

3. Mark the lace equally into eight, then gather. Mark the outer edge of the collar into eight also, then pin the lace all round, matching the marked points. Draw up to fit, distributing the gathers evenly, and stitch into place.

4. Cut the ribbon in half. Stitch behind each corner of the collar so that it can be crossed at the centre front and the ribbons tied in a bow at the back of the waist.

5. Follow the directions for making Charlotte's matching Mob Cap (page 33).

EMILY'S YELLOW ROSE PRINT DRESS

C lever Emily chose an extremely simple style to show off her pretty patterned fabric to the best advantage. She decided on a strong colour for her satin sash, but made her own braid from a subtle blend of the colours in the fabric. The longer skirt is very grown-up, hiding the lacy edges of her pantalettes.

– MATERIALS –

25cm (10in) cotton-type print fabric, 90cm (36in) wide
50cm (⅝yd) white lace, 10mm (⅜in) deep
70cm (¾yd) satin ribbon, 16mm (⅝in) wide
60cm (⅝yd) satin ribbon, 1.5mm (1/16in) wide, in EACH of THREE toning colours
50cm (½yd) matching bias binding
2 snap fasteners
Clear adhesive

———— · ————

1. Cut the bodice front once and the back and sleeve twice each. Cut a piece 24.5cm (9¾in) deep × 40cm (16in) wide for the skirt.

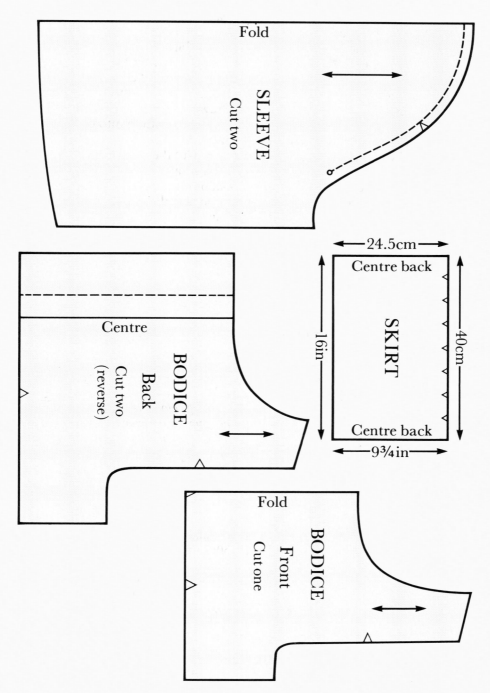

Fold

SLEEVE
Cut two

24.5cm

Centre back

16in

SKIRT

40cm

Centre back

9¾in

Centre

BODICE
Back
Cut two
(reverse)

Fold

BODICE
Front
Cut one

EMILY'S YELLOW ROSE PRINT DRESS

2. Follow the directions for Mary-Anne's Lace-trimmed Brown Dress (above), omitting the lace trimming.

3. If the neck binding doesn't lie flat, gather very close to the top edge with tiny stitches, and draw up slightly to the correct shape. Gather a 25cm (10in) length of lace and pin the top edge evenly along the *centre* of the binding: stitch into place, drawing up to fit.

4. Cut a 20cm (8in) length of 1.5mm (¹⁄₁₆in) ribbon in each colour, and make a plaited braid (see chapter 2). Glue over the top half of the neck binding, above the lace.

5. Stitch lace flat over sleeve binding to overlap the lower edge. Make plaited braid from 16cm (6½in) lengths of ribbon and glue over the top edge of the lace.

6. Fit wider ribbon around the waist for the sash, lower edge of ribbon level with the bottom of the bodice: stitch cut ends at centre back. Catch the lower edge across the front to hold in place, if necessary. Make a bow from 12cm (5in) ribbon (method A in chapter 2), using the remaining ribbon for streamers. Stitch at centre back.

EMILY'S FILMY STOLE AND MOB CAP

*E*very fashionable lady has a delicate stole to wear across her shoulders so that the ends float behind her when she walks. Emily made hers from a sheer striped ribbon, and she's rather proud of the result! Her mob cap echoes the yellow roses on her dress.

— MATERIALS —

Two 30cm (12in) diameter circles of white lawn-type fabric
1m (1yd) Sheer Multi-stripe ribbon, 23mm (⁷⁄₈in) wide
25cm (10in) single-face satin ribbon, 16mm (⁵⁄₈in) wide
30cm (12in) narrow round elastic
Clear adhesive

1. Cut the striped ribbon in half. Draw threads to fringe the cut ends.

2. Place the two lengths side by side and glue together, overlapping the edges about 1.5mm (¹⁄₁₆in).

3. Follow the directions for making Charlotte's Matching Mob Cap (page 33). (page 33)

LOUISA'S BIRTHDAY DOLL

*N*o wonder Louisa is so pleased with her birthday present! A new doll is always exciting – but this one, in her sugar pink taffeta bonnet, is quite the most enchanting the girls have ever seen. William is feeling just a little bit neglected!

– MATERIALS –

Turned paper ball, 30mm (1¼in) diameter, flesh colour (or paint with poster colour)
3 pipe cleaners (chenille stems), 16.5cm (6½in) long
Scrap of flesh felt
Polyester stuffing (or wadding or cotton wool)
7 strands Twilley's dark brown embroidery wool, 76cm (30in) long, OR any fine knitting yarn (for the hair)
12×50cm (4½×18in) light-weight white cotton-type fabric (for her dress)
10×20cm (4×8in) pale pink taffeta (for her bonnet)
1m (1yd) narrow white lace
50cm (½yd) pale pink lace, 10mm (⅜in) deep
60cm (¾yd) single-face Colonial Rose satin ribbon, 6mm (¼in) wide
20cm (¼yd) single-face Colonial Rose satin ribbon, 10mm (⅜in) wide
White cartridge-weight paper
Medium-weight card
Black fibre-tip pen, or black ink, etc
Dry stick adhesive
Clear adhesive

———— . ————

1. For the arms, bend two pipe cleaners in half, then place them together as diagram (a) overleaf and bind tightly at crosses to hold in position.

2. For each hand, cut the pattern twice in felt and oversew together with tiny stitches all round, leaving the straight edges open. Slip over the end of the arm, then stitch and bind tightly around the wrist to secure.

3. Bend another pipe cleaner in half and push the ends into the ball for the head (don't glue yet). Fit the arms between the body pipe cleaner, 5mm (¼in) below the head, and bind tightly (diagram (b)).

4. Wrap stuffing, wadding or cotton wool around the central pipe cleaner (as broken lines in diagram (b)), to pad out the body. Bind with thread to hold in place.

5. Cut a piece of white fabric 10cm (4in) deep × 15cm (6in) wide for her petticoat. Join the side edges to form the centre back seam, and turn to the right side. Stitch white lace so that it just overlaps the lower edge. Mark the top edge into four and gather. Fit on the doll, close under the arms, pinning the marked points at the sides and front and the seam at the back. Draw up gathers, distributing them evenly, and catch into place.

6. Cut another piece of white fabric, 9.5cm (3¾in) deep × 20cm (8in) wide for her skirt. Join the side edges to form the centre back seam, and turn to the right side. Stitch a row of pink lace so that it just overlaps the lower edge, with another row just overlapping the first one. Finish with a row of *very* narrow white lace (fold or cut narrow lace in half) along the top edge of the upper row of pink. Mark the top edge into four and gather. Fit on the doll, pinning the marked points as before, over the petticoat gathers: draw up and secure as for the petticoat.

7. Cut the bodice in white fabric: cut as indicated for the centre front opening, and cut away the centre circle for the neck. Fold in half (diagram (c)) and join the sleeve seams at each side of the notches, as shown, leaving 2cm (¾in) open at the centre. Turn under a tiny hem around the wrist edges and gather, but don't draw up. Turn to the right side and fit on the doll. Pin the centre front edges so that they *meet*, then cross-stitch

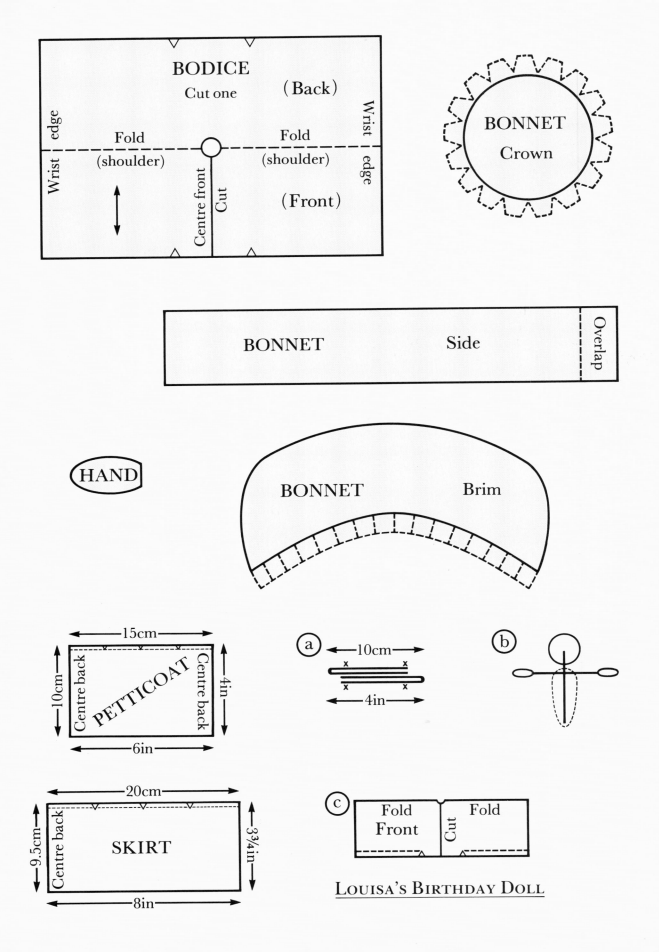

BODICE

Cut one

(Back)

Wrist edge

Fold (shoulder)

Wrist edge

Fold (shoulder)

Wrist

Centre front

Cut

(Front)

BONNET Crown

BONNET   Side   Overlap

HAND

BONNET   Brim

15cm

Centre back   Centre back

PETTICOAT

10cm

4in

6in

ⓐ 10cm

4in

ⓑ

20cm

Centre back

SKIRT

9.5cm

3¾in

8in

ⓒ Fold Front   Fold

Cut

LOUISA'S BIRTHDAY DOLL

neatly to hold together. Stitch *very* narrow lace over the join. Draw up the wrist gathers tightly and secure over tops of hands.

8. Glue the head onto the pipe cleaner. Make skeins of wool for the hair, adapting the directions for the hairstyles in chapter 3 as follows:
1st skein: Wind three strands of embroidery wool (or similar yarn) around a 10cm (4in) deep card: tie at each side with a single strand of wool. Remove from the card and tie the centre loosely with matching thread. Glue the centre to the top of the doll's head, taking the ends down at each side (as illustrated) and round to the back, gluing as you go: knot the ties together at the nape of the neck.
2nd skein: Wind three strands around a 9cm (3½in) deep card: tie and remove as before, but tie the centre *tightly*. Glue the centre close behind the centre of the 1st skein, then take down to cover the back of the head, glueing into place: knot ties and tuck the ends neatly underneath.

9. Gather 10cm (4in) white lace and draw up tightly around the neck; join at back. Gather 8cm (3¼in) *very* narrow white lace and draw up tightly around each wrist.

10. Circle the waist gathers with 10mm (⅜in) wide ribbon, joining at the back. Make a bow from 7cm (2¾in) of the same ribbon, but bind the centre with 6mm (¼in) ribbon, folded in half (method A in chapter 2). Make ties from 15cm (6in) of the narrower ribbon. Glue ties and bow to back of sash, over the join.

11. Cut the bonnet brim, side and crown (ignore broken lines) once each in paper. Using the dry stick adhesive, glue the crown to pink taffeta: cut the fabric beyond the edge of the paper and snip the surplus into tiny tabs as broken lines. Glue the overlap on the side to form a circle, then fit the crown over one end and glue the tabs down neatly to hold it in place. Cover the outside of the brim with taffeta and trim level with the paper. Then cover the inside in the same way, but leave a surplus of fabric around the inner curve, and snip it into tiny tabs, as broken lines. Glue these tabs neatly round inside the back of the bonnet. Cut a strip of taffeta, using the pattern for the side, and glue it over the paper, trimming the edge level with the crown. Glue *very* narrow lace around the edge of the brim. Glue 6mm (¼in) ribbon around the bonnet, behind the brim. Fit the bonnet on the doll (glue if necessary). Make a bow from 3.5cm (1⅜in) of the same ribbon (method A in chapter 2, but don't bind the centre): glue under the chin. Make a many-petalled rose from the remaining 6mm (¼in) ribbon, and glue at centre front, over the band and brim.

IMPROVING OCCUPATIONS

*T**he girls spend every morning improving their minds and practising their artistic skills. Charlotte reads aloud while Emily embroiders a sampler in perfect cross-stitch; Louisa knits a striped coat for William and Mary-Anne paints his portrait. They are all wearing variations of the same basic Kate Greenaway shift dress.*

Mary-Anne is wearing the same brown dress that she wore for the birthday breakfast in chapter 5. She has removed her shawl collar to reveal the low, round neck, into which she was tucked a single rose.

Emily wears the same dress, too – but without her matching stole. If you remember, she had fallen in love with the yellow rose printed fabric, and decided on this simple shift dress to show it off to the best advantage. Louisa and Mary-Anne were impressed with Emily's good taste. So, not to be outdone, *they* went hunting for some pretty prints, too.

Louisa found a tiny design in two shades of green on a cream ground. She used the darker shade of green for her sash and bias binding, then trimmed the neck and sleeves with 16mm (⅝in) deep cream lace (a little deeper than Emily's), and used two strands of green ribbon and one of cream to make the plaited braid.

Charlotte couldn't resist purple rosebuds scattered over a paler ground. She chose a purple sash, and matched the

Note: Directions for the Velvet Upholstered Chair, Matching Padded Footstool, Flowery Triple-folding Screen and Small Side Table are in chapter 13.

light fabric for the binding. She thought black lace would be very sophisticated (the same depth as Emily's): then she picked up the three shades of colour in the rosebud and plaited Light Orchid, Grape and Purple ribbons for her braid trimming.

Determined to improve just a little on Emily's original, the other girls decided they wanted a more dramatic effect at the back. So they made their sashes from 16mm (⅝in) wide ribbon, just like Emily's, but then used a wider version of the same ribbon for the bow and streamers. If you want to do the same, you will need only 25cm (¼yd) of the narrower ribbon for the sash, plus 50cm (½yd) 23mm (⅞in) wide: use 15cm (6in) for the bow, and the remainder for the streamers.

The girls were surprised and delighted when all their dresses looked so different. Just find an attractive printed fabric with a tiny design, and follow the directions for Emily's Yellow Rose Print Dress (chapter 5), adapting the trimmings to reflect your fabric, as they have done. The result will be a charming frock, so typical of Kate Greenaway that she might have drawn it for you.

CHAPTER 7

GOING SHOPPING

*I*t's a lovely spring morning and the girls are going shopping. Louisa and Mary-Anne greet the sunshine in clear spring colours, with bonnets to match. But there's a cool breeze, so each is playing safe with a warm-cover-up over her cotton dress.

LOUISA'S SPRIGGED WHITE DRESS

*L*ouisa admired Mary-Anne's Lace-trimmed Brown Dress so much that she borrowed the pattern and made it up for summer in a fresh white cotton, sprigged with tiny flowers in yellow and peach. Then she cleverly matched the colours for a frilly shoulder cape and a wide-brimmed hat crowned with roses.

– MATERIALS –

25cm (¼yd) printed cotton-type fabric, 90cm (36in) wide
1m (1yd) white lace, 10mm (⅜in) deep
50cm (½yd) matching bias binding
2 snap fasteners

————— . —————

1. Use the pattern for Mary-Anne's Lace-trimmed Brown Dress (see chapter 5).

2. Follow the directions as given for Mary-Anne's Lace-trimmed Brown Dress, trimming the sleeves as instructed, but omitting the lace around the neck and hem.

3. Gather a 30cm (12in) length of lace, then pin it evenly round the neck, the top edge of the lace level with the *lower* edge of the binding: draw up to fit and stitch neatly. Gather another 30cm (12in) length of lace and pin it round the neck,

level with the *top* edge of the binding: draw up and oversew into place.

LOUISA'S FRILLY SHOULDER CAPE

*T*his sweet little cape matches the yellow flowers on her dress, and is trimmed with lots of delicate ruffled lace and fastened with a single rose.

– MATERIALS –

25×35cm (10×14in) spotted voile (or similar fabric)
1.20m (1¼yd) lace, 25–30mm (1–1¼in) deep
25cm (10in) single-face satin ribbon, 6mm (¼in) wide (in contrast colour, for the rose)
Snap fastener

————— . —————

1. Cut the pattern twice, noting the straight of fabric arrows: to make cutting easier, trace the pattern onto folded paper, then open out and place flat on your fabric.

2. Join the two pieces along the inner and outer curved edges, leaving the straight edges open. Using pinking shears, clip the seams carefully, then turn to the right side. Top-stitch the edges neatly, close to the seams.

3. Gather each pair of straight raw edges: draw up tightly and secure.

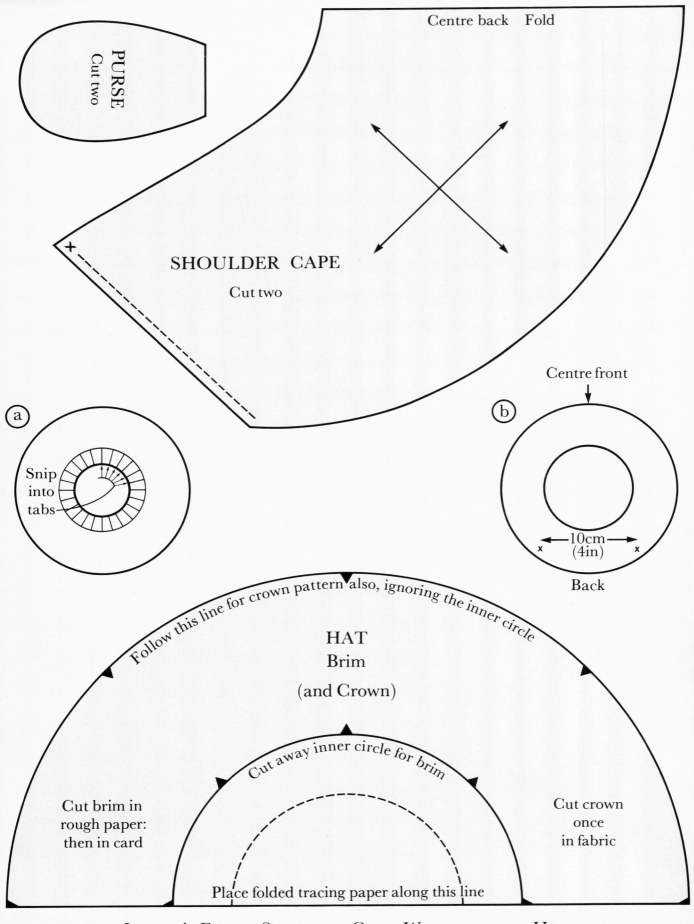

PURSE
Cut two

Centre back   Fold

SHOULDER CAPE

Cut two

+

(a)
Snip into tabs

(b)
Centre front

10cm
(4in)

x   x

Back

Follow this line for crown pattern also, ignoring the inner circle

HAT
Brim

(and Crown)

Cut away inner circle for brim

Cut brim in
rough paper:
then in card

Cut crown
once
in fabric

Place folded tracing paper along this line

LOUISA'S FRILLY SHOULDER CAPE, WIDE-BRIMMED HAT
AND PURSE

4. Mark an 80cm (30in) length of lace into eight, then gather – about 7–8mm (¼in) below the straight top edge. Mark the outer edge of the cape into eight, beginning and ending at the front corners (x), then pin the lace so that the gathering stitches are just above the edge of the cape and the lower edge of the lace overlaps. Draw up to fit, distributing the gathers evenly, and stitch into place, turning under the cut ends neatly. Repeat with a 40cm (15in) length of lace for the inner edge, but this time position it so that the top edge of the lace overlaps the edge of the cape, and the lower edge of the lace falls downwards in the same direction as the previous piece. Turn under the cut ends and gather tightly.

5. Make a rather flat ribbon rose (see chapter 2), and stitch to one front corner. Stitch the snap fastener underneath to close over the other front corner.

LOUISA'S WIDE-BRIMMED HAT

*H*er elegant hat is in the same shade as the peach flowers on her dress, with dramatic contrasting roses to match the one on her cape.

– MATERIALS –

25×60cm (10×24in) spotted voile (or similar fabric)
23×32cm (9×12½in) thin white card
60cm (¾yd) lace edging, 10mm (⅜in) deep
1.30m (1½yd) single-face satin ribbon, 16mm (⅝in) wide (in contrast colour for the roses)
30cm (12in) double-face satin ribbon, 10mm (⅜in) wide (for the streamers)
Dry stick adhesive
Clear adhesive

———— · ————

1. Cut the brim pattern in a piece of rough stiff paper and check on the doll for size: the inner circle should fit her head loosely. (Keep the rough pattern for future use.) Cut the brim again in plain white card, adjusting the size of the inner circle if necessary.

2. Using the dry stick adhesive, spread glue evenly over the surface, and cover one side of the brim with fabric: trim the inner and outer edges level with the card. Cover the underside in the same way, and trim the outer edge level again, but cut away only a 6cm (2½in) diameter circle in the centre (broken line on the pattern): snip the surplus into tiny tabs (as diagram (a)).

3. Cut a strip of card 1.5×32cm (½× 12½in) for the sides of the crown. Curve into a circle the same size as the inner circle of the brim (fit inside to measure): glue the join. Fit over the top of the brim, then bring the tabs up from underneath and glue them neatly all round inside the side strip.

4. For the crown, cut the brim pattern again in tracing paper, *ignoring the centre circle*. Cut the pattern in fabric, marking notches, then gather all round the edge.

5. Mark the inner circle notches on your original rough paper brim: place this over the brim of your hat and mark the notches all round the side strip. Remove the paper and fit the fabric circle over the side strip, drawing up to fit and matching the notches: pin at each marked point (raw edge of fabric level with lower edge of card). Catch into place all round, distributing the gathers evenly.

6. Cut another side strip in thin card, this time 1×32cm (⅜×12½in). Cut a strip of fabric 2.5×33cm (1×13in) and place right side down. Glue the card strip down the centre of the fabric, using stick adhesive, then fold each long edge over and glue to the back of the card. Trim the ends level. Glue this strip around the crown, over the gathers, the lower edge of the card level with the top of the brim and the join at the back.

7. Glue lace around the edge of the brim, pulling it taut so that it folds over as illustrated, the lower edge of the lace overlapping the underside of the brim.

8. Use the single-face ribbon to make three roses (as chapter 2), one from 50cm (20in) ribbon, and two from 40cm (16in) ribbon. Glue the larger rose at the centre front of the hat, over the covered strip, with a smaller one at each side.

9. Make a small bow at the centre of the double-face ribbon (method B in chapter 2). Glue the bow over the join in the strip at the back of the crown, the streamers hanging down over the brim: trim the cut ends in an inverted V-shape.

10. Bend the sides of the brim down towards the face to give the shape illustrated. If the brim will not retain this shape, hold it in place with a thread across the back between crosses (as diagram (b)) about 6–7mm (¼in) from the edge and 10cm (4in) apart, drawing it up underneath the brim to measure 3–4cm (1¼–1½in).

MARY-ANNE'S BROWN SPRIGGED DRESS

For her shopping trip to town, Mary-Anne chose a short-sleeved version of her Lace-trimmed Brown Dress. The pretty sprigged cotton is perfect when teamed with her smart new Spencer Jacket – and when worn in this way, needs no trimming.

– MATERIALS –

25cm (¼yd) printed cotton-type fabric, 70cm (30in) wide
50cm (½yd) matching bias binding
2 snap fasteners

1. Use the pattern for Mary-Anne's Lace-trimmed Brown Dress (chapter 5), noting the shorter cutting line for the sleeve.

2. Follow the directions for Mary-Anne's Lace-trimmed Brown Dress, omitting the lace trim.

MARY-ANNE'S SPENCER JACKET

There are often cool breezes just around the corner on the sunniest spring day, so Mary-Anne tops her dress with a fashionable Spencer Jacket in spicy orange with a military trimming of dark brown braid. Mary-Anne is planning to make a winter version too, omitting the lace frills and using a wider braid trim.

– MATERIALS –

18×30cm (7×12in) felt
1m (1yd) very narrow silky braid
1m (1yd) white lace, 10mm (⅜in) deep (optional)
2 snap fasteners
Clear adhesive

1. Cut the back once and the front and sleeve twice each.

2. Join the front pieces to the back at each shoulder.

3. Mark the centre at the top of each sleeve, then gather between the circles. Fit the sleeve into the armhole, matching side edges and notches, and centre top with the shoulder seam. Draw up the gathers to fit, distributing them evenly between the marked points: stitch. When both sleeves are in place, join the side seams of the sleeve and jacket. Turn to the right side.

4. Glue braid neatly round the neck, right front and lower edges, and the cuffs.

5. Mark 35cm (14in) lace into eight and gather. Mark the neck edge into eight and pin the lace just inside, matching the marked points: draw up to fit and stitch.

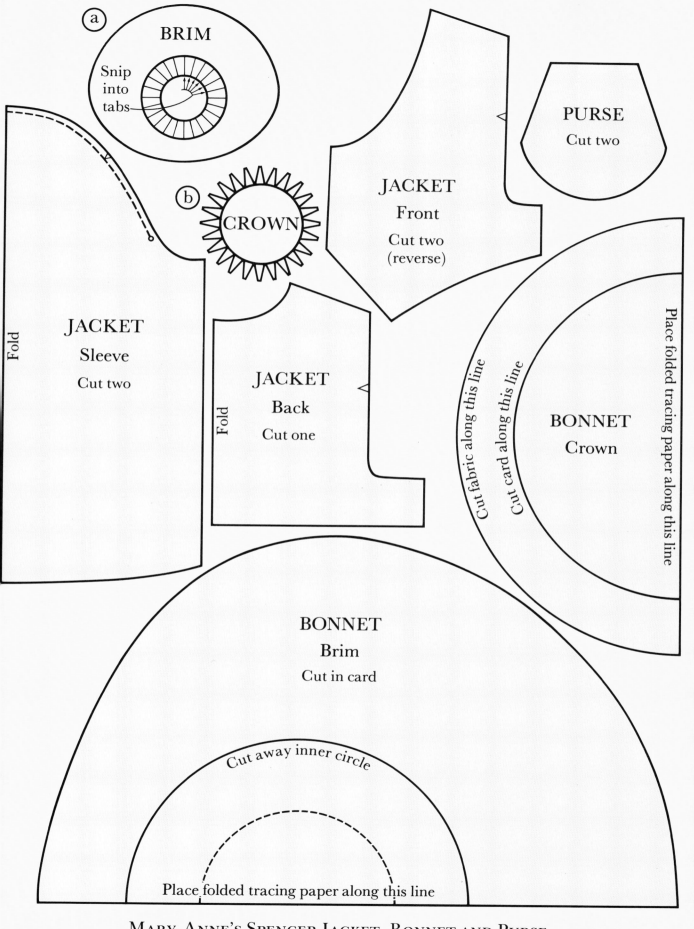

MARY-ANNE'S SPENCER JACKET, BONNET AND PURSE

Then fold the lace over the edge of the jacket and catch above the top of the braid, so the frill stands out slightly.

Trim each sleeve with 25cm (10in) lace as the neck, but omit the final stage, so that the frill extends straight down from the cuff.

MARY-ANNE'S BROWN SPRIGGED BONNET

The bonnet is a flattering shape, made in the same fabric as her dress: but a plain fabric in a toning colour could be just as alluring, especially if it were trimmed with tiny flowers.

– MATERIALS –

25×80cm (10×32in) cotton-type fabric
30cm (12in) square of thin white card
60cm (¾yd) lace edging, 10mm (⅜in) deep
1m (1yd) Sheer Multi-stripe ribbon, 23mm (⅞in) wide
30cm (12in) satin ribbon, 3mm (⅛in) wide (for roses)
Dry stick adhesive
Clear adhesive

———— · ————

1. Cut the brim and crown patterns in white card, as well as two strips, each 5× 30cm (2×12in) for the sides of the crown. Curve one of the strips into a circle the same size as the inner circle of the brim (fit inside to measure): glue the join.

2. Spread dry stick adhesive evenly over one side of the brim and then cover with fabric: trim the inner and outer edges level with the card. Cover the underside in the same way, and trim the outer edge level again, but cut away only a 5cm (2in) diameter circle in the centre (broken line on the pattern): snip the surplus into tiny tabs (diagram (a)).

3. Fit the prepared circle over the top of the brim, then bring the tabs up from underneath and glue them neatly all round inside the side strip.

4. Cut a circle of fabric for the crown, as pattern: place right side down and glue the card circle in the centre. Snip tiny V-shaped notches all round (as diagram (b)) to make tabs, then place over the top edge of the sides and glue the tabs neatly down all round.

5. Cut a strip of fabric 8×32cm (3× 12½in): place right side down and glue the second strip of card down the centre, using stick adhesive. Then fold each long edge over and glue to the back of the card. Trim the ends level. Glue around crown, over the first strip, with the join at the back.

6. Glue lace around the edge of the brim, pulling it taut so that it folds over as illustrated, the lower edge of the lace overlapping the underside of the brim.

7. Cut a 70cm (24in) length of the striped ribbon: take the middle across the centre of the crown and down over each side, catching to hold in place at the point where the crown joins the brim. To make each rosette, overlap and glue the cut edges of a 15cm (6in) length of the same ribbon to form a circle, then gather one edge and draw up tightly. Catch one at each side over previous stitches, as illustrated.

8. Make two roses as chapter 2 from 15cm (6in) satin ribbon, and glue one in the centre of each rosette.

LOUISA AND MARY-ANNE'S PURSES

Just large enough to carry their money, a clean lace handkerchief and some peppermints, both reticules are made in exactly the same way: only the shape and trimmings are different.

– MATERIALS –

6×8cm (2½×3in) piece of felt (Louisa)
5×10cm (2×4in) piece of felt (Mary-Anne)
7cm (3in) narrow gold or silver braid
Small gold or silver bead for clasp
12cm (5in) satin ribbon, 1.5mm (¹⁄₁₆in) wide,
   to match felt, for the handle
Satin ribbon, 3mm wide, to trim (see step 5)
Cotton wool (or stuffing)
Clear adhesive

———— · ————

1. Cut the pattern twice in felt.

2. Oversew together all round, leaving the straight top edge open. Push a little cotton wool inside to fill out the base.

3. Glue the ends of the narrow ribbon inside the top, against the seams, to form a handle.

4. Glue braid across the top edges, on both sides, then glue bead at the centre.

5. Louisa's reticule is trimmed with a rose made from 8cm (3in) ribbon (see chapter 2), and a bow made from 6cm (2½in) ribbon (method B in chapter 2).
Mary-Anne's has three roses, the centre one made from 10cm (4in) ribbon, and the other two from 8cm (3in) ribbon.

MARY-ANNE'S SHOPPING BASKET

*T*he basket can be any size and shape you
wish – just design it as you stitch. For a
very simple flower basket, like the one
illustrated in chapters 5 and 8, simply work
a flat circle, then curve the sides up and add
a handle. Use ordinary garden raffia: it is
much cheaper than craft raffia, and the
natural colour is just right for basket-
making.

– MATERIALS –

Garden raffia
Matching sewing thread

1. Use two really thick strands together, or three or four thinner ones. Knot them together at one end, then wrap the strands of raffia in a circle round the knot, keeping them smooth and close: oversew with matching thread to hold in place (figure a). Continue in this way, winding the raffia round and round, oversewing to the previous round: keep the circle absolutely flat – like a mat – and work until it is 5cm (2in) in diameter.

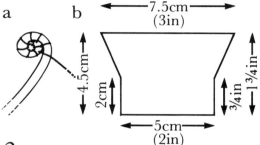

a   b

2. Sew the next round at right-angles to the previous round, so that you are stitching it to the top of the 'mat'. Continue to work the sides absolutely straight until the basket is 2cm (¾in) deep. Now begin to sew at an angle, so that each round takes the sides of the basket outwards (figure b). Work until the basket is about 4.5cm (1¾in) deep and roughly 7.5cm (3in) diameter at the top: finish off neatly.

3. Thread a thick strand of raffia (or two thinner ones) into a tapestry or darning needle, and form the handle by stitching the raffia through each side of the basket and looping it over the top: make the handle as long as you like, although 15cm (6in) is a good length. Take the raffia over about ten times, keeping the strands absolutely even, then bind them all together with the rest of the strand, winding it tightly and closely round and round the handle. Finish off all the ends neatly inside the basket.

4. Push and pull gently into shape, so the top is slightly oval, measuring about 6×8cm (2½×3in).

CHAPTER 8

SUMMER GARDEN PARTY

*M*ary-Anne is entertaining Emily to tea in the garden on an afternoon in high summer. Both, of course, are wearing their prettiest frocks. Emily is charming in lilac voile with a tiny white flock spot and matching poke bonnet, whilst Mary-Anne wears an enchanting dress in white lawn patterned with tiny pink daisies, her picture hat adorned with a gigantic cabbage rose.

EMILY'S LILAC AND TARTAN DRESS

*T*his *very fashionable day dress and matching bonnet are ideal for visiting friends to take tea in the garden on a summer afternoon. Emily chose pale lilac voile contrasted with a dashing green-and-blue tartan sash tied in an enormous bow at the back. The dainty sleeves are quite the latest thing, but if you prefer to make a simpler version, just substitute the sleeve pattern, and follow the directions, for Charlotte's Dark Flowered Dress in chapter 5.*

– MATERIALS –

50cm (½yd) lilac spotted voile (or similar fabric), 90cm (36in) wide
25×35cm (10×14in) thin white card
60cm (¾yd) very narrow black lace (or braid), 3mm (⅛in) deep
2m (2¼yd) white lace, 10mm (⅜in) deep
85cm (1yd) white guipure lace daisies (or braid), 10–15mm (½in) wide
1.10m (1¼yd) Tartan Taffeta ribbon, 25mm (1in) wide
40cm (½yd) matching tartan ribbon, 10mm (⅜in) wide
15cm (6in) bias binding
50cm (½yd) narrow round elastic

3 snap fasteners
Dry stick adhesive
Clear adhesive

1. Cut the bodice front once, and the bodice back and the upper and lower sleeve twice each. Cut a piece 24cm (9½in) deep × 40cm (16in) wide for the skirt.

2. Join the bodice front to the back pieces at each shoulder.

3. Gather the bottom edge of the upper sleeve: pin to the top edge of the lower sleeve, matching notches. Draw up the gathers to fit, distributing them evenly, and stitch. Mark the centre at the top edge of the upper sleeve and gather between the circles. Fit the sleeve into the armhole of the bodice, matching side edges and notches, and centre top with the shoulder seam. Draw up the gathers to fit, distributing them evenly between the marked points, and stitch. Clip curves. When both sleeves are in place, join the side seams of the sleeves and bodice.

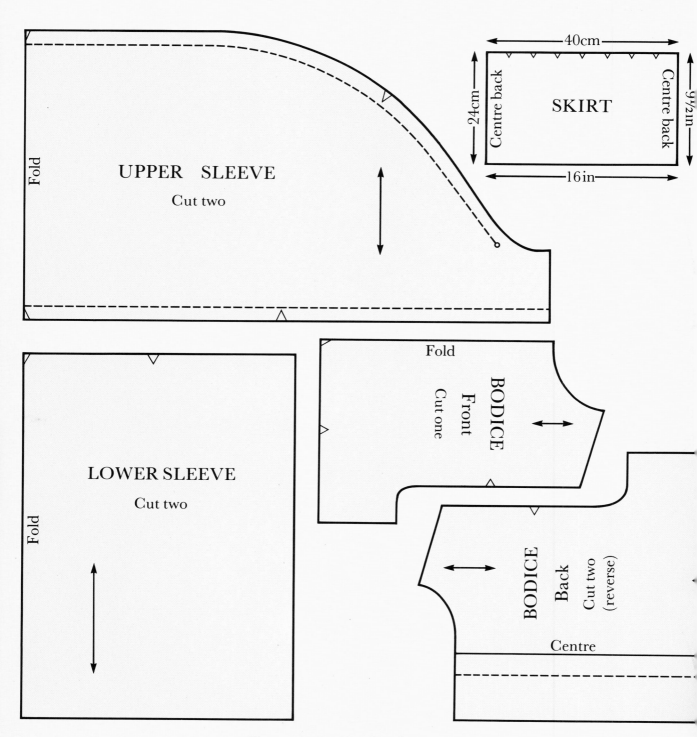

UPPER SLEEVE

Cut two

Fold

SKIRT

40cm

24cm

Centre back

Centre back

9½in

16in

LOWER SLEEVE

Cut two

Fold

BODICE

Front

Cut one

Fold

BODICE

Back

Cut two (reverse)

Centre

EMILY'S LILAC VOILE DRESS

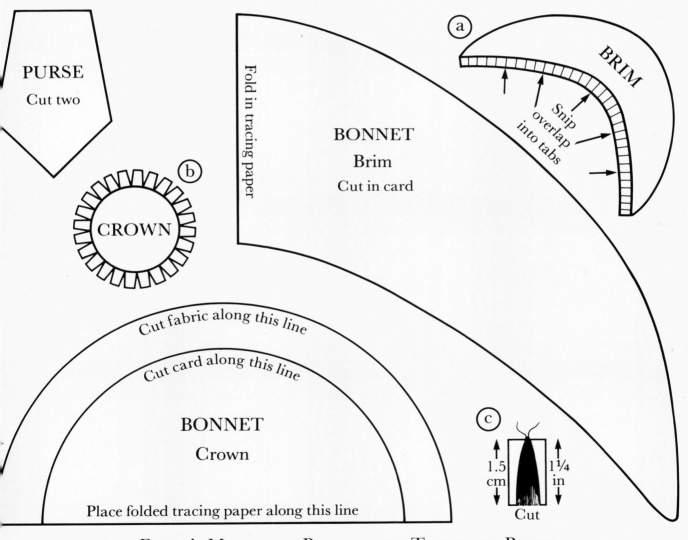

PURSE
Cut two

BRIM

ⓐ

Snip
overlap
into tabs

ⓑ
CROWN

Fold in tracing paper

BONNET
Brim
Cut in card

Cut fabric along this line

Cut card along this line

BONNET
Crown

ⓒ

1.5
cm

1¼
in

Cut

Place folded tracing paper along this line

EMILY'S MATCHING BONNET AND TASSELLED PURSE

4. Turn up a 1cm (⅜in) hem around the lower edge of the sleeve: turn to the right side and stitch narrow black lace just above the hemline. Stitch lace also around the top edge of the lower sleeve, immediately below the gathers. Turn to the wrong side and catch narrow round elastic behind the bands of black lace, 12cm (5in) at the top and 10cm (4in) at the wrist, making a herringbone-stitch over the top of the elastic (check the elastic runs freely under the thread): draw up the elastic to fit, and knot the ends.

5. Mark the top edge of the skirt equally into eight, then gather, beginning and ending 2cm (¾in) from the side edges. Pin to the lower edge of the bodice, matching marked points to notches and seams. Draw up to fit, and stitch, distributing the gathers evenly. Turn the gathers up inside and top-stitch close to the lower edge of the bodice. Join the centre back seam of the skirt, leaving 5cm (2in) open at the top. Turn under the centre back edges of the bodice as broken line, and stitch: turn under and stitch the edges of the skirt opening to correspond.

6. Bind the neck edge, then stitch white lace on top to form a tiny stand-up collar.

7. Fold the ribbon in half lengthways, and catch around the waist, lower edge of ribbon level with lower edge of bodice: finish the ends neatly at the back. Make a bow (method A in chapter 2), using a 15cm (6in) length of ribbon bound with a scrap folded into three. Make streamers from 30cm (12in) ribbon. Stitch at the back of the bodice.

8. Stitch snap fasteners to the back opening at neck, centre and waist.

9. Turn up a 2cm (¾in) hem, then trim the right side with three rows of lace, about 3mm (⅛in) apart.

– EMILY'S MATCHING BONNET –

10. Trace the bonnet brim and crown on to thin card and cut out. Cut a strip 7×32cm (2¾×12½in) for the sides of the crown.

11. Rub dry stick adhesive all over one side of the brim, then place smoothly down on the wrong side of your fabric: cut level all round the outer edge, but leave a 1cm (⅜in) overlap along the inner curve. Snip this overlap into tiny tabs (diagram (a)), turn them neatly over the edge and glue to the underside of the card. The side you have covered is the *outside* of the brim. Cover the inside in exactly the same way, but leave a 1.5cm (½in) overlap along the inner curve: snip the surplus into tiny tabs, but don't glue them down.

12. Curve the side strip round into a cylinder and glue the short edges, overlapping 2cm (¾in). Cut a strip of fabric 10×32cm (4×12½in). Wrap the fabric round the card, overlapping each edge 1.5cm (½in), and glue the overlap: then turn the surplus over each long edge and glue inside (use clear adhesive for this).

13. Cut a circle of fabric for the back of the crown as the pattern, then glue the card circle to the wrong side with the glue stick. Snip the surplus into V-shaped tabs (diagram (b)), then fold them neatly over the edge and glue underneath.

14. Very carefully glue the tabs round the brim inside the crown, keeping the edges of the brim and sides of the crown absolutely level. Then oversew the back circle to the other edge of the crown.

15. Glue white lace around the outer edge of the brim, pulling it taut so it turns inward over the edge. Then glue daisies or braid over the straight edge of the lace, and also around the back edge of the crown, over the stitches.

16. Glue a band of wide tartan ribbon around the crown, close to the inner edge of the brim. Cut the narrow ribbon in half and glue the ends inside the crown, to form ties.

EMILY'S TASSELLED PURSE

– MATERIALS –

6×8cm (2½×3in) deep lilac felt
6cm (2½in) narrow gold or silver braid
Small gold or silver bead for clasp
10cm (4in) satin ribbon, 1.5mm (¹/₁₆in) wide (to match felt) for the handle
30cm (12in) satin ribbon, 3mm (⅛in) wide, in a paler shade of lilac
Stranded embroidery cotton to match 3mm (⅛in) ribbon
Mother-of-pearl flower sequin (optional)
Cotton wool (or stuffing)
Clear adhesive

———— · ————

1. Cut the pattern twice in felt.

2. Oversew together all round, leaving the straight top edges open. Push a little cotton wool inside to fill out the base.

3. Glue the ends of the narrow ribbon inside the top, against the seams, to form a handle.

4. Glue braid across the top edges, on both sides, then glue bead at the centre.

5. Make the tassel by winding embroidery cotton ten times around a 1.5cm (½in) deep piece of card. Slip a single thread through and tie the top edge tightly (diagram C), then cut the bottom edge neatly. Bind the tassel tightly with a single strand, just below the top. Stitch to hang freely from the bottom point of the purse.

6. Make three roses from 10cm (4in) lengths of 3mm (⅛in) wide ribbon (see chapter 2). Glue to the front of the purse

and, if liked, add tiny leaves cut from the petals of a flower sequin.

MARY-ANNE'S GARDEN PARTY DRESS

*M*ary-Anne hunted in all her favourite shops for a really light-weight fabric which would be cool and fresh for a hot summer afternoon. She found a very fine cotton lawn – a drift of white, scattered with pink daisies. Her full-length dress has frothy lace frills round the low neck and sleeves, a broad sash and three layers of crisp lace holding out the hem of the full skirt.

– MATERIALS –

25cm (10in) light-weight lawn-type fabric, 90cm (36in) wide
3.20m (3½yd) white lace, 10mm (⅜in) deep
70cm (¾yd) Colonial Rose double-face satin ribbon, 16mm (⅝in) wide
50cm (½yd) Colonial Rose single-face satin ribbon, 6mm (¼in) wide
50cm (½yd) matching bias binding
3 snap fasteners

———— · ————

1. Cut the bodice front once and the back and sleeve twice each. Cut a piece 25cm (10in) deep × 60cm (24in) wide for the skirt.

2. Follow the directions for Mary-Anne's Lace-trimmed Brown Dress (chapter 5), but omit all trimming and snap fasteners.

3. If the neck binding doesn't lie flat, gather very close to the top edge with tiny stitches and draw up slightly to correct the shape. Gather a 30cm (12in) length of lace, then pin it evenly round the neck, the top edge of the lace level with the *lower* edge of the binding: draw up to fit and stitch neatly. Gather another 30cm (12in) length of lace and pin it round the neck, level with the *top* edge of the binding: draw up and oversew into place.

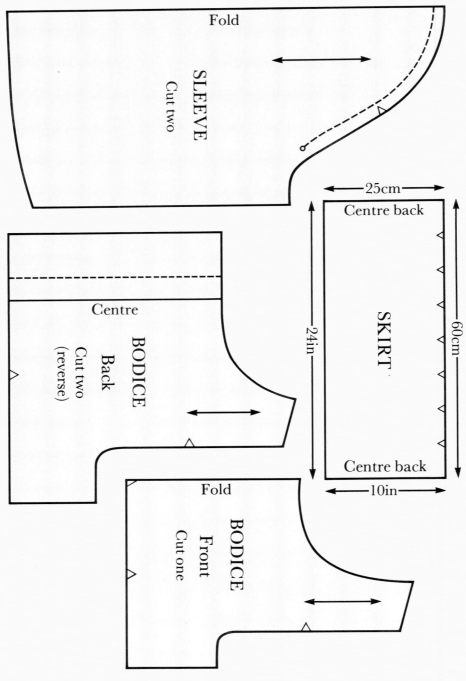

Mary-Anne's Garden Party Dress

4. For each sleeve, gather an 18cm (7in) length of lace, then pin it evenly round, the top edge of the lace just over the folded edge of the binding, so the rest overlaps the lower edge of the sleeve: draw up and stitch neatly. Gather another 18cm (7in) length and pin this with the top edge over the binding and level with the fabric: draw up and stitch.

5. Stitch a row of flat lace around the hem, the lower edge about 1cm (3/8in) above the bottom of the skirt. Stitch two more rows above, about 3mm (1/8in) apart.

6. Stitch snap fasteners to the back opening at neck and waist.

7. Fit wider ribbon around the waist for her sash, the lower edge of the ribbon level with the bottom of the bodice: stitch the cut ends at the centre back. Catch the lower edge across the front, if necessary. Make a bow from 12.5cm (5in) wider ribbon (method A in chapter 2), using the remaining ribbon for streamers. Stitch at the centre back over the sash.

8. Gather the narrower ribbon along the centre and draw up tightly for her neckband. Stitch a snap fastener at the ends to secure.

MARY-ANNE'S PICTURE HAT, PARASOL AND STOLE

A rose-trimmed taffeta hat with an enormous brim, a fashionable stole and a frilly parasol complete the romantic illusion for Mary-Anne's garden party.

– MATERIALS –

25×70cm (10×27in) rose pink taffeta
20×60cm (8×24in) thin white card
10×18cm (4×7in) thin- to medium-weight white paper
75cm (7/8yd) white lace, 30mm (1 1/4in) deep
75cm (7/8yd) pink lace, 10mm (3/8in) deep
30cm (12in) Colonial Rose single-face satin ribbon, 16mm (5/8in) wide
70cm (3/4yd) Colonial Rose single-face satin ribbon, 10mm (3/8in) wide
25cm (1/4yd) Colonial Rose single-face satin ribbon, 6mm (1/4in) wide
30cm (12in) EACH Sherbert Pink and Light Pink single-face satin ribbon, 10mm (3/8in) wide
50cm (1/2yd) Sheer Multi-stripe pink ribbon, 23mm (7/8in) wide, for the hat
1m (1yd) Sheer Multi-stripe pink ribbon, 23mm (7/8in) wide, for the stole
Bamboo pick (skewer) OR very thin stick OR dried corn stalk, etc, 20cm (8in) long
Pink bead, about 10mm (3/8in) diameter
Dry stick adhesive
Clear adhesive

———— · ————

1. Cut the brim and crown patterns in white card, and a 3×32cm (1 1/8×12 1/2in) strip for the sides of the crown. Curve the strip into a circle the same size as the inner circle of the brim (fit inside to measure): glue the join.

2. Using dry stick adhesive, spread glue evenly over the surface and cover one side of the brim with fabric: trim the inner and outer edges level with the card. Cover the underside in the same way, and trim the outer edge level again, but cut away only a 6cm (2 1/4in) diameter circle in the centre (broken line on the pattern): snip the surplus into tiny tabs (as diagram (a)).

3. Fit the prepared circle over the top of the brim, then bring the tabs up from underneath and glue them neatly all round inside the side strip.

4. Cut a circle of fabric for the crown, as pattern: place right side down and glue the card circle in the centre. Snip tiny, V-shaped notches all round (as diagram (b)) to make tabs, then place over the top edge of the sides and glue the tabs neatly down all round.

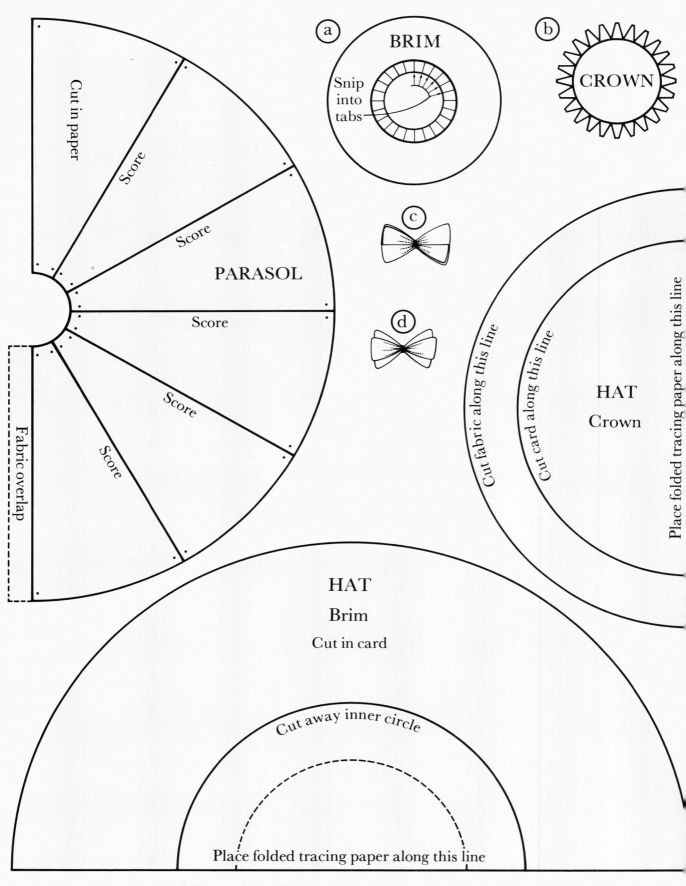

MARY-ANNE'S PICTURE HAT AND PARASOL

5. Cut a strip of fabric 3×32cm (1⅛× 12½in) and glue round the sides of the crown (with the join just off centre front so that it will be hidden behind the trimming).

6. Glue pink lace around the edge of the brim, pulling it taut so it folds over as illustrated, the lower edge of the lace overlapping the underside of the brim.

7. Fold a 40cm (16in) length of 10mm (⅜in) ribbon in half for the streamers: gather across the fold, draw up tightly and stitch to the back of the hat, at the point where the crown joins the brim. Fit a band of 16mm (⅝in) ribbon around the crown, joining at the front as before.

8. Make three bows from 16cm (6in) lengths of sheer ribbon (method A in chapter 2, but don't bind the centres with ribbon). Bind two together (as diagram (c)) then bind the third on top (as diagram (d)). Glue to the crown over joins in fabric and ribbon.

9. Glue the cut edges of a 23cm (9in) length of white lace to form a circle, then gather the straight edge and draw up tightly to make a rosette.

10. Make a rose from 30cm (12in) of 10mm (⅜in) Colonial Rose ribbon (see chapter 2). Then join a 30cm (12in) length of Sherbert Pink ribbon behind and continue to make petals in the same way. Repeat with a 30cm (12in) length of Light Pink ribbon. Stitch the rose to the centre of the lace rosette. Then glue to the centre of the sheer bows.

11. Make another small rose from 25cm (9in) of 6mm (¼in) ribbon and glue at the back, over the top of the streamers.

12. Curve the brim down slightly at the back and front (as illustrated).

13. Cut the parasol in paper and mark the lines accurately. Then rub dry stick adhesive all over the back and glue smoothly to fabric. Cut the fabric level with the edge of the paper, but leave a surplus overlapping one straight edge, as indicated by the broken line on pattern.

14. Score each line (using a blunt knife and ruler), then fold and crease sharply, the fabric *inside* each fold. Open out flat again.

15. Gather 50cm (½yd) of white lace along the straight edge. Pin evenly around the edge of the outer curve: draw up the gathers to fit, and stitch into place.

16. Turn over and, re-creasing each fold as you come to it, catch them together at the top and bottom by taking one stitch through each fold as indicated by the dots on pattern: don't draw up, but leave the thread on the right side.

17. Curve round and glue the overlapping fabric inside the other straight edge to join. Then draw up the gathers tightly at top and bottom, and secure.

18. Fit the bamboo pick (or similar stick) through the centre and glue to hold in place.

19. Glue the cut ends of a 15cm (6in) length of pink lace, then gather along the *centre* and draw up tightly around the base of the parasol, catching into place.

20. Glue the bead on top of the handle.

21. Follow the directions for making Emily's Filmy Stole (chapter 5).

CHAPTER 9

WINTER VISITING

*L*ouisa, Charlotte and William trudge through the snowdrifts – all warm as toast in their colourful winter outfits. Louisa chose Kate Greenaway's favourite shade of green for hers; Charlotte's is a rich violet trimmed with heliotrope. William's tartan jacket is a mixture of both.

LOUISA'S OLIVE GREEN CLOAK

*F*elt is ideal for this cosy cloak and shoulder cape. If you can't find a suitable braid, make your own from satin ribbon (see chapter 2). Materials are given separately for the cloak and bonnet, in case you prefer to make them in different colours.

– MATERIALS –

30cm (12in) felt, 90cm (36in) wide
OR three 30cm (12in) squares
1.50m (1¾yd) braid, 10mm (⅜in) wide
5 snap fasteners
Clear adhesive

1. Cut a piece of felt 28×60cm (11×24in): if using squares, join two to form the centre back seam. Mark the centre of the top edge with a pin. Then pin-mark the top edge three times at each side of the first (centre) pin, each pair of pins 7.5cm (3in) apart.

2. Trace and cut the dart pattern seven times. Pin darts to the wrong side of the felt, top edges level and arrows pointing to the pins: mark the edges of the darts. Fold and pin each dart as broken line on pattern, then cut only the *darts marked A (see diagram) just inside the marked line*, as indicated on the pattern. Oversew the cut edges together, tapering to a neat point at the tip.

3. Cut the two darts marked B (on the diagram) along the outside marked line. Join the cut edges for 1cm (⅜in) only at the top (above notches) to form armholes. On right side, glue braid round edge of armhole, beginning and ending at top.

4. Turn up and sew a 1cm (⅜in) hem along the lower edge. Turn 2cm (¾in) along each front edge over to the *right side* and oversew the top edge: turn this hem to the inside and stitch neatly into place.

5. Gather the top edge – excluding the 2cm (¾in) hem at each end – and draw up the *gathers* to measure 11cm (4¼in).

6. Cut the cape as the pattern: either in two pieces (with a join at the centre back), or in three pieces (with joins on the shoulders).

7. Mark the top edge of the cape into four, as notches, then gather and draw up to measure 11cm (4¼in). With the *right* side of the cape to the *wrong* side of the cloak, pin the gathered top edges, matching the marked points on the cape to the centre back and shoulders (darts B). Oversew together, distributing the gathers evenly. Turn cape to right side.

Note: Directions for William's Winter Jacket are in chapter 12.

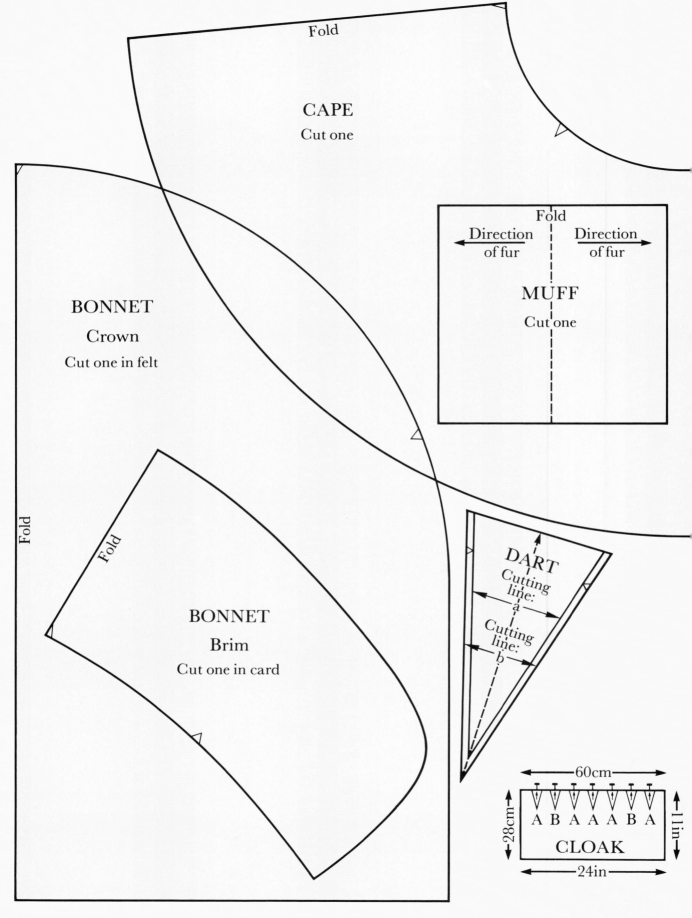

Fold

CAPE

Cut one

Fold

Direction of fur ← → Direction of fur

MUFF

Cut one

BONNET

Crown

Cut one in felt

Fold

Fold

BONNET

Brim

Cut one in card

DART

Cutting line: a

Cutting line: b

60cm

↑↓ A B A A A B A ↑↓

28cm   11in

CLOAK

24in

LOUISA'S OLIVE GREEN CLOAK, MATCHING BONNET AND MUFF

8. Stitch two snap fasteners at the neck, so the front edges overlap about 2.5cm (1in). Then sew three more at 6cm (2½in) intervals down the front.

9. Glue braid down the centre front and around the hem of the cloak and the edge of the cape.

LOUISA'S MATCHING BONNET AND MUFF

– MATERIALS –

25×50cm (10×20in) felt
OR two 25cm (10in) squares
6×12cm (2⅜×4¾in) cream fur fabric
10×25cm (4×10in) thin card
40cm (½yd) braid, 10mm (⅜in) wide
1.20m (1⅜yd) single-face satin ribbon, 6mm (¼in) wide
30cm (12in) single-face satin ribbon, 10mm (⅜in) wide
30cm (12in) cream lace, 25mm (1in) deep
Cotton wool, wadding or tissue
Dry stick adhesive (optional)
Clear adhesive

———— · ————

1. Cut the bonnet brim in card. Rub dry stick adhesive (or spread clear adhesive) over one side, and stick to felt: cut the felt to leave about 2mm (1/16in) around the outer edge, and 3mm (⅛in) along the inner edge. Glue the other side of the card to felt and cut in the same way. Oversew the *outer* edges together.

2. Cut the crown in felt and mark notches. Gather all round the sides and top, close to the edge. Right sides together, pin the gathered edge to the inner edge of the brim, matching notches: draw up the gathers to fit and oversew neatly, distributing the gathers evenly.

3. Gather the lace and pin inside the brim, drawing up to fit: oversew the gathered edge along the previous stitching line. Gather the cut ends and draw up tightly at each side.

4. Gather the straight back edge. Fit the bonnet on the doll, pinning at each side so that the brim is in the correct position: draw up the gathers to fit (not *too* closely). Cut a 2cm (¾in) wide strip of felt the same length as the back edge, and use to bind the gathers, distributing them evenly so that it forms a stay-strip.

5. Glue braid over the edge of the brim.

6. Run the centre of a 60cm (24in) length of narrow ribbon across the back of the brim, against the gathers, with the ends hanging down equally at each side to form ties. Stitch securely at each end of the brim.

7. Make a bow from 10cm (4in) of the wider ribbon (method A in chapter 2). Stitch just above the centre of the brim.

8. Push a little cotton wool, wadding or tissue inside the crown to hold the shape.

9. Cut the muff in felt. On the wrong side rule a line, lengthways down the centre, as broken line on pattern. Right side inside, join the two short ends.

10. Cut two pieces of fur fabric, each 12cm (4¾in) long × 3cm (1³⁄₁₆in) wide, with the direction of the fur going *across* the width (so it overlaps one long edge). Glue the two strips of fur around the felt, edges level at the centre, so the fur overlaps each side of the muff.

11. Glue braid over the centre join. Trim the front with a bow made as in step 7, but using only 8cm (3in) of the wider ribbon.

12. Cut two 30cm (12in) lengths of the narrow ribbon. Fold each to form three equal loops. Stitch the tops of the loops together, then stitch or glue one bunch inside each end of the muff, so they extend and hang down as illustrated.

CHARLOTTE'S VIOLET COAT

*C*harlotte chose a glowing colour for her stylish high-waisted winter coat. Then she got quite carried away trimming her hat with heliotrope ribbons and a riot of satin roses in every shade from pink to purple. She searched high and low for a braid to match her coat: when she couldn't find what she wanted, she decided to make her own from double plaited ribbon in a slightly darker shade. But if you prefer to use purchased braid, and can't find a suitable colour, black would be very smart on this particular coat.

– MATERIALS –

30cm (12in) violet felt, 90cm (36in) wide
6.50m (7yd) Mulberry satin ribbon, 1.5mm (¹⁄₁₆in) wide
OR 80cm (⅞yd) braid, 8–10mm (⅜in) wide
25cm (¼yd) Helio single-face satin ribbon, 6mm (¼in) wide
25cm (¼yd) Mulberry satin ribbon, 3mm (⅛in) wide (optional)
6 snap fasteners
Clear adhesive

———————— . ————————

1. Cut the bodice back, the skirt back and the collar once each, and the bodice front, skirt front and sleeve twice each.

2. Join the bodice front pieces to the back at each shoulder.

3. Mark the centre at the top of each sleeve, then gather between the circles. Fit the sleeve into the armhole, matching side edges and notches, and centre top with the shoulder seam.

4. Join the skirt fronts to the back at each side.

5. Gather the top edge of the skirt between the circles. Right sides together, pin to the lower edge of the bodice, matching notches and side seams. Draw up to fit and join, distributing the gathers evenly. Turn to the right side.

6. Fit the coat on the doll to determine length. Turn up and stitch the hem accordingly, about 2cm (¾in).

7. Turn under the front edges as broken line on pattern, and stitch.

8. Right sides together, oversew one long edge of the collar around the neck edge, the collar overlapping a fraction at each end. Right side inside, fold the collar in half as broken line, and join the short ends. Turn to the right side and slip-stitch the lower edge along the previous stitching line, inside the coat.

9. Stitch snap fasteners down the centre front opening, one inside the collar, two on the bodice and three on the skirt (see crosses on pattern).

10. Make two pieces of plaited braid (see chapter 2) for the centre front edge, using 40cm (15in) lengths of narrow Mulberry ribbon: make two pieces for the collar, using 25cm (10in) lengths of ribbon: and two pieces for each sleeve, using 20cm (8in) lengths of ribbon. Glue side by side as illustrated. Alternatively, trim the coat with purchased braid.

11. Make three bows from 8cm (3in) lengths of 6mm (¼in) Helio ribbon (method B in chapter 2). Glue to the front of the bodice, over the trimming, as illustrated. Make three tiny roses (see chapter 2) from 8cm (3in) lengths of 3mm (⅛in) Mulberry ribbon, and glue at the centre of the bows (the roses may be omitted, if preferred).

CHARLOTTE'S MATCHING HAT AND MUFF

– MATERIALS –

25cm (10in) violet felt, 90cm (36in) wide
25cm (10in) square thin card
75cm (⅞yd) black lace, 10mm (⅜in) deep
1.10m (1¼yd) Mulberry satin ribbon, 1.5mm (¹⁄₁₆in) wide
25cm (10in) Plum single-face satin ribbon, 6mm (¼in) wide
60cm (¾yd) Helio single-face satin ribbon, 6mm (¼in) wide
2m (2¼yd) Helio single-face satin ribbon, 10mm (⅜in) wide: PLUS 50cm (⅝yd) EACH in Purple, Grape and Light Orchid
40cm (½yd) Plum single-face satin ribbon, 12mm (½in) wide
20cm (¼yd) Helio satin ribbon, 16mm (⅝in) wide
Cotton wool, wadding or tissue
Dry stick adhesive (optional)
Clear adhesive

———— · ————

1. Cut the hat brim in card: mark the overlap at *each* end on *both* sides. Rub glue stick (or spread adhesive) over one side, omitting the overlap at each end, and stick to felt: cut the felt to leave about 2mm (¹⁄₁₆in) around the outer edge, and 3mm (⅛in) around the inner edge. Glue the other side of the card to felt and cut in the same way. Glue the card overlap. Then trim away the felt to leave a 5mm (¼in) overlap on each side, and glue. Oversew the *outer* edges of the felt together. Mark notches around inner edge.

2. Cut the crown in felt and mark notches. Gather all round, close to the edge. Draw up the gathers so the crown is bowl-shaped (right side inside); place the brim over the crown (as diagram (a)). Pin gathered edge of crown to inner edge of the brim, matching notches: draw up to fit and oversew together. Push the crown through the brim, turning it to the right side.

3. Stitch lace round the edge of the brim, slightly overlapping.

4. Gather across the centre of a 20cm (8in) length of 16mm (⅝in) Helio ribbon: draw up tightly, fold in half and catch together to form streamers. Stitch top of streamers to centre back of hat at the point where the crown joins the brim, so the ribbons fall over the join in the brim.

5. Make a rose (see chapter 2) from 25cm (10in) of 10mm (⅜in) Helio ribbon: glue over top of streamers. Make another rose from 40cm (16in) of 12mm (½in) Plum ribbon: glue at centre front of hat, over the crown/brim join. Make six more roses from 25cm (10in) lengths of 10mm (⅜in) Helio ribbon: *pin* one at each side of the centre Plum rose. Make two similar roses in Purple ribbon: pin behind the previous two, followed by two more Helio ones. Make two roses in Grape ribbon: pin behind the previous two followed by two more in Helio. Make two in Light Orchid ribbon: pin between the previous two and the centre back rose. Adjust positions and then glue into position around the crown.

6. Push a little cotton wool, wadding or tissue inside the crown to hold the shape.

7. Cut the muff in felt. Join the short ends and turn to the right side. Stitch lace just overlapping each end. Make two pieces of plaited braid (see chapter 2) from 18cm (7in) lengths of 1.5mm (¹⁄₁₆in) Mulberry ribbon. Glue over the inner edge of the lace. Make a bow (method B in chapter 2) from 12.5cm (5in) of 10mm (⅜in) Helio ribbon and stitch at the centre front. Glue a rose on top, made from 20cm (8in) of 6mm (¼in) Plum ribbon.

8. Cut two 30cm (12in) lengths of 6mm (¼in) Helio ribbon. Fold each to form three equal loops. Stitch the tops of the loops together, then stitch or glue one bunch inside each end of the muff, so they extend and hang down as illustrated.

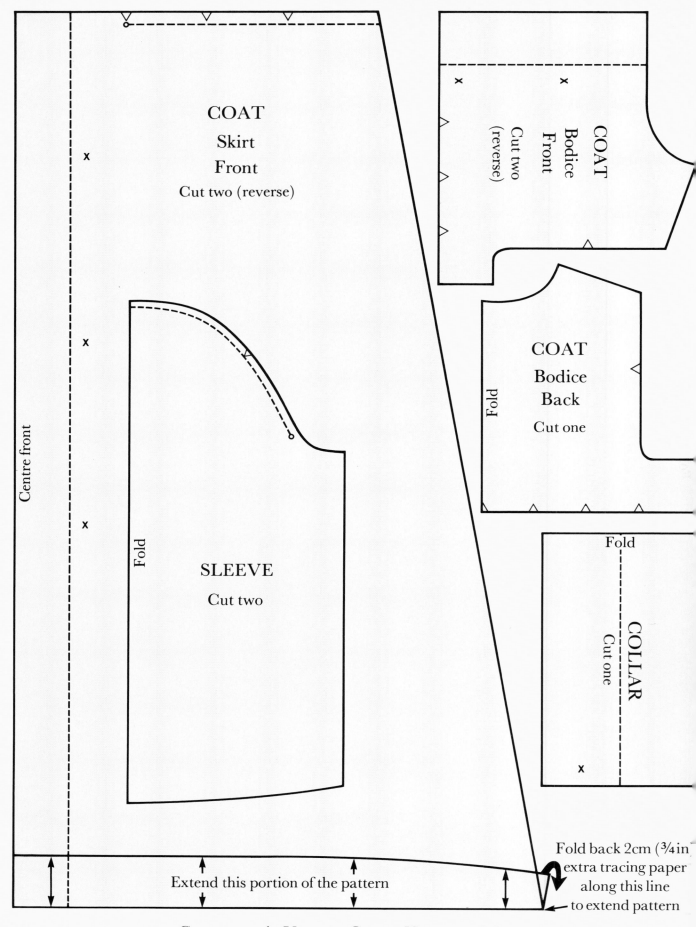

COAT
Skirt
Front
Cut two (reverse)

COAT
Bodice
Front
Cut two
(reverse)

COAT
Bodice
Back
Cut one

Centre front

Fold

SLEEVE
Cut two

Fold

Fold

COLLAR
Cut one

Extend this portion of the pattern

Fold back 2cm (¾in)
extra tracing paper
along this line
to extend pattern

CHAROTTE'S VIOLET COAT, HAT AND MUFF

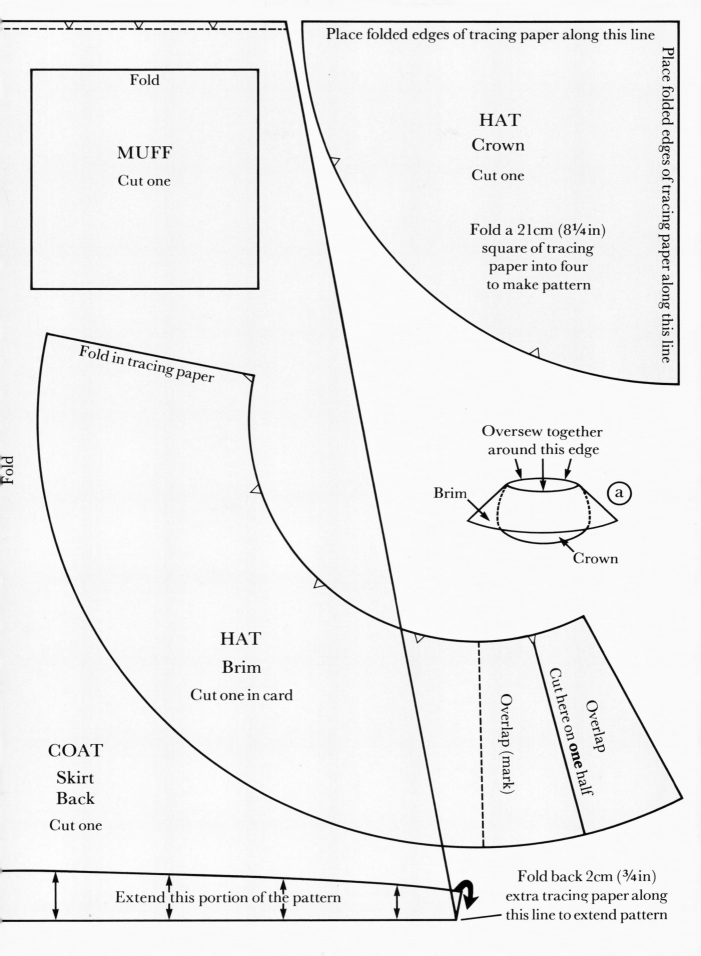

Fold

MUFF

Cut one

Place folded edges of tracing paper along this line

HAT

Crown

Cut one

Fold a 21cm (8¼ in)
square of tracing
paper into four
to make pattern

Place folded edges of tracing paper along this line

Fold

Fold in tracing paper

Oversew together
around this edge

Brim

(a)

Crown

HAT

Brim

Cut one in card

Overlap (mark)

Overlap
Cut here on **one** half

COAT

Skirt
Back

Cut one

Extend this portion of the pattern

Fold back 2cm (¾ in)
extra tracing paper along
this line to extend pattern

CHAPTER 10

PARTY-GOING

*E*mily has been invited to a party. She's been practising her dance
steps for days, and now everyone wants to help her with her
beautiful new satin gown.

EMILY'S OLD-FASHIONED BALLGOWN

*E*mily could dance all night in this
nostalgic creation of midnight blue and
sparkling champagne, trimmed with toning
lace and pink roses. Don't *use an expensive
dress-weight satin for this softly draped
gown because it will be too stiff and heavy.
Instead, look for a good-quality lining satin,
which is much softer, and drapes well. And
don't attempt to cut the bodice without first
backing the satin with an iron-on
interlining: this will prevent the tiny seams
fraying, and give you firm edges to bind for
the sleeves and neckline.*

– MATERIALS –

35cm (½yd) deep blue lining satin, 90cm
   (36in) wide
30×45cm (12×18in) champagne lining satin
Two 30cm (12in) diameter circles of deep
   cream silk-type lining fabric
13×60cm (5×24in) light-weight iron-on
   non-woven interlining (Vilene)
1m (1yd) blue-grey lace, 10mm (⅜in) deep
1.40m (1½yd) deep cream lace, 10mm (⅜in)
   deep
15cm (6in) Antique Blue single-face satin
   ribbon, 10mm (⅜in) wide
1m (1yd) Antique Blue single-face satin
   ribbon, 6mm (¼in) wide
2m (2¼yd) Antique Blue satin ribbon,
   1.5mm (¹⁄₁₆in) wide

Note: Directions for the Pearl-framed Mirror and
the Curtained Wardrobe are in chapter 13.
Directions for Louisa's chemise and pantalettes,
and Mary-Anne's petticoat are in chapter 4.

2.50m (3yd) Colonial Rose single-face satin
   ribbon 10mm (⅜in) wide
15cm (6in) Colonial Rose single-face satin
   ribbon, 6mm (¼in) wide
15cm (6in) black velvet ribbon, 5mm (¼in)
   wide
50cm (½yd) matching blue bias binding
30cm (12in) narrow round elastic
9 snap fasteners
Clear adhesive

———— · ————

1.   Cut the underskirt in champagne
satin, 29cm (11½in) deep × 45cm (18in)
wide. Cut the overskirt in blue satin,
20cm (8in) deep × 90cm (36in) wide.
Then cut a piece of blue satin 13cm (5in)
deep × 60cm (24in) wide and back it with
iron-on interlining: from this cut the
bodice front once and the bodice back
and sleeve twice each.

2.   Follow the directions for Mary-
Anne's Lace-trimmed Brown Dress
(chapter 5), treating the champagne
underskirt as the skirt, but omitting all
the lace trimming.

3.   Gather the straight edge of a 35cm
(14in) length of blue-grey lace and pin it
evenly round the neck, the straight edge
along the *centre* of the binding: draw up to
fit and stitch into place, distributing the
gathers between the pins. Plait three
30cm (12in) lengths of 1.5mm (¹⁄₁₆in)
ribbon (see chapter 2) and glue over the
top half of the binding, above the top
edge of the lace.

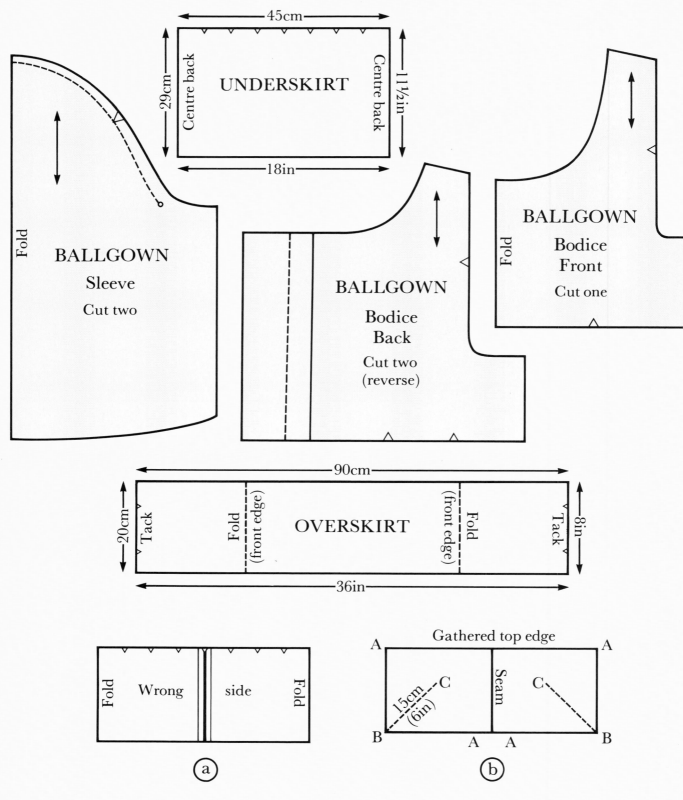

45cm

29cm | Centre back | **UNDERSKIRT** | Centre back | 11½in

18in

Fold | **BALLGOWN** | Sleeve | Cut two

BALLGOWN | Bodice Back | Cut two (reverse)

Fold | **BALLGOWN** | Bodice Front | Cut one

90cm

20cm | Tack | Fold (front edge) | **OVERSKIRT** | Fold (front edge) | Tack | 8in

36in

Fold | Wrong | side | Fold

ⓐ

Gathered top edge

A | A | Seam | A | A
C | C
15cm (6in)
B | A | A | B

ⓑ

EMILY'S OLD-FASHIONED BALLGOWN

4. Stitch blue-grey lace around the edge of each sleeve, so almost all the lace overlaps below. Then stitch another row of lace above, half-overlapping the first one. Finally, plait three 18cm (7in) lengths of ribbon and glue over the straight edge of the upper row of lace.

5. Stitch a row of cream lace around the hem of the underskirt, 1cm (⅜in) above the edge: stitch two more rows above first one, about 3mm (⅛in) apart.

6. To make the overskirt, *pin* the two short edges together, then mark this edge 5cm (2in) from each end. Stitch the seam between each end and the marked points. Then tack the 10cm (4in) in the centre (see the pattern diagram). Press the seam open. Fold the fabric, right side inside, as diagram (a). Stitch along the lower edge. Then mark the top edge equally into eight, and gather. Measure the waist of your doll, *over* the dress, and cut a piece of 6mm (¼in) ribbon the same length plus 5mm (¼in). Mark this also into eight, then pin it over the gathers matching the marked points, the lower edge of the ribbon level with the gathering thread. Draw up the gathers to fit, distributing them evenly, and stitch the ribbon securely over the top of the gathers (*above* the gathering thread) to hold them in place. Remove the tacking thread and turn to the right side. Top-stitch very close to the lower edge on the inside of the overskirt (the side with the seam), trying to let your stitches show as little as possible on the outside. Neaten the top gathered edge in the same way. Mark diagonal lines on the inside of the overskirt as diagram (b) (*note*: to make the diagram easy to understand, the top edge is shown *flat*, although it has of course already been gathered): to find the diagonals, fold the fabric from each corner B so that the side edge is level with the lower edge, matching points A, then mark C on the foldline 15cm (6in) from B. Mark the line between B and C, then

open out and gather: draw up tightly and secure, then bring the corner (B) to the inside and catch it over point C.

7. To fix the overskirt to the dress, stitch snap fasteners inside each front corner and at the centre back: stitch the corresponding halves to the underskirt, directly below the bodice, the two front fasteners close together. Fix the overskirt to the dress, then mark the position of another fastener at each side, below the side seam of the bodice. Stitch these into position. Finally, make a bow (method B in chapter 2) from 15cm (6in) of 10mm (⅜in) ribbon and stitch it to one top corner of the overskirt so that it is centred over the join when overskirt is in place.

8. Make seven similar bows from 10cm (4in) lengths of 6mm (¼in) ribbon. Stitch one to the centre front of the underskirt, over the top row of lace. Then stitch four more at 3.5cm (1⅜in) intervals above it. Glue the two remaining bows to the sleeves, over the plaited braid.

9. Make a rose (see chapter 2) from 15cm (6in) of 6mm (¼in) pink ribbon. Stitch to centre front of neckline.

10. Make ten more roses from 25cm (10in) lengths of 10mm (⅜in) ribbon. Follow the directions for Charlotte's Matching Mob Cap (chapter 5), but before threading the elastic through the channel, fix the roses into position as follows: mark the channel with a pin at the centre front. Then pin a rose over the channel 2.5cm (1in) each side of the centre pin. Pin four more roses at each side of the first two, at 5cm (2in) intervals. Sew the roses into position over the channel, but take care to stitch *each side* of it to avoid impeding the elastic. Thread the elastic through and draw up to fit the doll's head.

11. Make the velvet ribbon into a neckband, fastening with a snap fastener.

CHAPTER 11

TIME FOR BED

E*mily had a wonderful time at the party and it was after midnight before she had finished telling the others all that had happened. Now she is ready for bed in her warm winter nightgown (you can see Louisa wearing the summer version in Chapter 4). Charlotte waits her turn to kiss a sleepy William goodnight before she tucks him up in his basket. Her négligé is very feminine, and makes her feel extremely grown-up.*

CHARLOTTE'S LOVERS' KNOTS AND LACE NÉGLIGÉ

*A*t the end of a busy day Charlotte puts on a flattering négligé with a demure neckline, brushes her hair and says her prayers. She chose a pale blue lawn dotted with white daisies, trimmed with layers of crisp white lace and lots of true lovers' knots. For really chilly winter nights when she wants to toast her toes by the fire, Charlotte plans to use the same pattern for a dressing gown in soft wool, trimmed with plaited ribbon braid.

– MATERIALS –

30cm (12in) light-weight lawn-type fabric, 90cm (36in) wide
1.70m (2yd) lace, 10mm (⅜in) deep
85cm (1yd) single-face satin ribbon, 6mm (¼in) wide
40cm (½yd) satin ribbon, 3mm (⅛in) wide
40cm (½yd) bias binding
7 snap fasteners

———— · ————

Note: Directions for the Roses and Lace Dressing Table and Stool, the Mirror and accessories, and the Rosebud and Ribbons Table are in chapter 13.

1. Cut the bodice front and sleeve twice each, and the bodice back once. Cut a piece of fabric 30cm (12in deep × 60cm (24in) wide for the skirt.

2. Join the bodice front pieces to the back at each shoulder.

3. Mark the centre at the top of each sleeve, then gather between the circles. Fit the sleeve into the armhole, matching side edges and notches, and centre top with the shoulder seam. Draw up the gathers to fit, distributing them evenly between the marked points: stitch. Clip curves. When both sleeves are in place, join the side seams of the sleeve and bodice.

4. Mark the top edge of the skirt 1.5cm (½in) from each side edge. Then mark the top edge, *between these two marks*, equally into sixteen. Gather, beginning and ending at the first two marks.

5. Right sides together, pin to the lower edge of the bodice, matching the side edges, and all the marked points on the skirt to the notches and side seams on the bodice. Draw up the gathers to fit, distributing them evenly between the

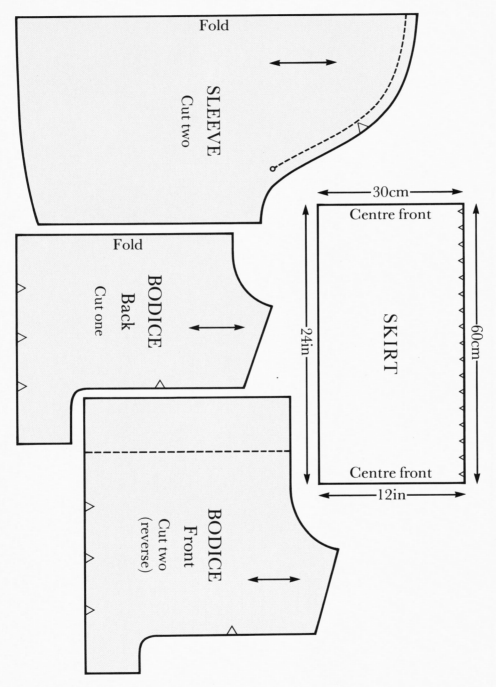

Fold

SLEEVE
Cut two

Fold

BODICE
Back
Cut one

BODICE
Front
Cut two
(reverse)

30cm

Centre front

SKIRT

60cm

24in

Centre front

12in

CHARLOTTE'S LOVERS' KNOTS AND LACE NÉGLIGÉ

pins, and stitch. Turn to the right side, fold the gathers *up* inside and then top-stitch neatly round the lower edge of the bodice.

6. Bind the lower edge of each sleeve, turning the full width of the binding up inside the sleeve. Stitch lace round the edge of each sleeve so almost all of it overlaps below. Then stitch two more rows of lace above, each half-overlapping the previous one.

7. Turn under and stitch the front edges of the bodice, as indicated by broken line on pattern: continue to turn under an equivalent amount down the front edges of the skirt.

8. Stitch 6mm (¼in) ribbon around the waist (it should be sufficient if you stitch it at the centre front, turning the ends inside, and then catch it under the sleeves and at the centre back).

9. Bind the neck, folding the binding in half over the raw edge.

10. Stitch lace down the *right* front edge, slightly overlapping. Then stitch a second row alongside it, with the outer edge in the opposite direction and the straight edge *over* the first one.

11. Stitch lace around the neck, the outer edge facing up to overlap the folded top edge of the binding, and the straight edge *halfway* down the binding. Gather a 20cm (8in) length of lace and then stitch it, with the outer edge facing down, over the lower edge of the binding, distributing the gathers evenly all the way round. Stitch 3mm (⅛in) ribbon around the neck, over the straight edges of the lace.

12. Stitch snap fasteners to the bodice at neck, centre and waist, and then four more at 5cm (2in) intervals down the front of the skirt.

13. To make a lovers' knot, tie a knot at the centre of a length of ribbon: then make another one on top. Make three from 8cm (3in) lengths of 3mm (⅛in) ribbon. Stitch at the neck, centre and waist (over the snap fasteners). Make four more from 10cm (4in) lengths of 6mm (¼in) ribbon: stitch these down the front of the skirt, *between* each pair of snap fasteners. Make two more from 6mm (⅛in) ribbon and stitch one over the top edge of the lace at the centre of each sleeve. Trim the cut ends in an inverted V-shape.

14. Fit the garment on the doll to determine length, then turn up the hem and stitch.

Louisa's Frilly Summer Nightgown and Matching Nightcap

(illustrated in chapter 4)

A romantic neckline, elbow-length sleeves, double layers of ruffled lace and satin ribbons make this the nightgown of Louisa's dreams. She looks lovely in ice blue cotton lawn, trimmed with deeper blue ribbons and drifts of snowy white lace. Louisa feels more like waltzing than going to sleep: but when she does *fall into bed, a frilly nightcap keeps her curls in place on the pillow.*

– MATERIALS –

40cm (½yd) light-weight lawn-type fabric, 90cm (36in) wide
6×23cm (2½×9in) heavy-weight non-woven interlining (Vilene or equivalent)
2m (2¼yd) lace, 15–20mm (½–¾in) deep: select a design through which you can slot 1.5mm (1⁄16in) ribbon
50cm (½yd) lace, 10mm (3⁄8in) deep (for nightcap)
10cm (4in) satin ribbon, 6mm (¼in) wide
50cm (½yd) satin ribbon, 3mm (1⁄8in) wide
80cm (1yd) satin ribbon, 1.5mm (1⁄16in) wide
70cm (¾yd) matching bias binding
25cm (¼yd) narrow round elastic
Snap fastener

———— • ————

1. Cut two pieces of fabric 30cm (12in) deep × 25cm (10in) wide for the back and front of the nightgown. Trace the pattern for the armhole and cut away this section at the top corners of each fabric piece (see diagram). Cut the (summer) sleeve, and the nightcap brim and back, twice each.

2. Join the nightgown side seams. Join each sleeve seam. Right sides together, and seams matching, stitch the underarm section of each sleeve (below the circles) into an armhole. Mark the centre top of each sleeve and the centre front of the skirt. Make a 6cm (2½in) slit for the centre back opening (see line on diagram): bind both edges, then make a tiny pleat to neaten the base, turning one bound edge back to close over the other. Pin the top corners of the opening together, overlapping correspondingly.

3. Gather across the top edge of the front. Gather round the top edge of each sleeve. Gather across each side of the back. Gather the front only again, 1.5cm (5⁄8in) below the first row, for the waistline. Right side *inside*, fit the nightgown on the doll and pin the tops of the armhole seams to the figure in the correct position for the neckline of the finished garment. Draw up each set of neckline gathers and secure, so that the neck fits neatly. Draw up the waist gathers. Remove the nightgown from the doll and bind the neck edge, distributing the gathers evenly as you do so. Stitch a snap fastener at the top of the back opening.

4. Mark 35cm (14in) lace into four, then gather and pin around the neckline, marked points at centre front and shoulders: stitch into place, over the gathers but close against the lower edge of the binding. Repeat with 30cm (12in) of lace, this time stitching it to the upper (folded) edge of the binding.

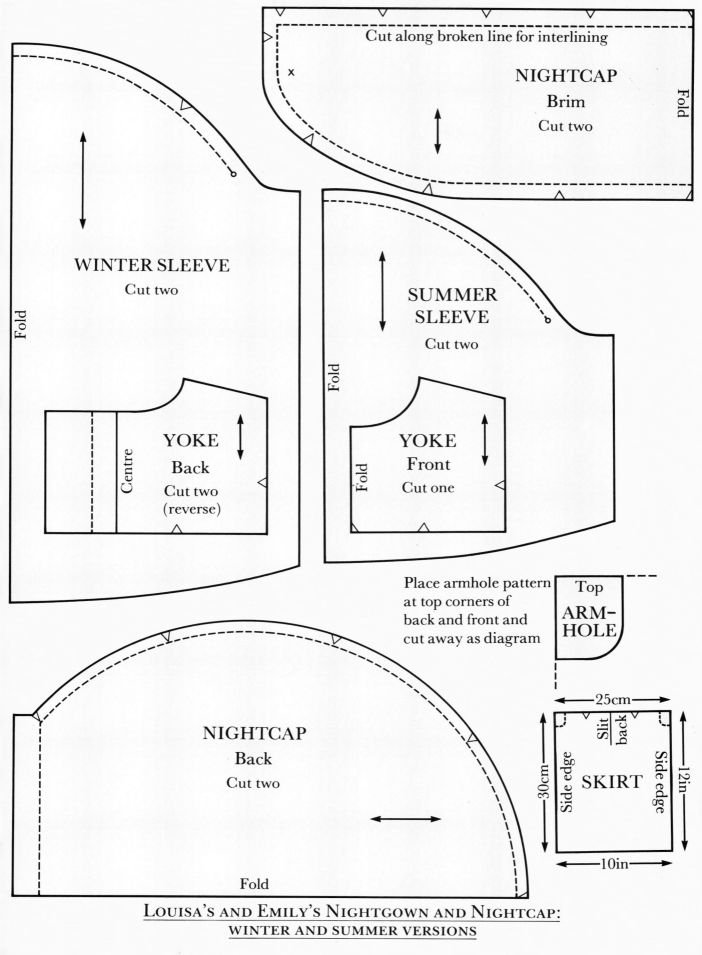

Cut along broken line for interlining

NIGHTCAP

Brim

Cut two

Fold

WINTER SLEEVE

Cut two

Fold

YOKE

Back

Cut two
(reverse)

Centre

**SUMMER
SLEEVE**

Cut two

Fold

Fold

YOKE

Front

Cut one

Place armhole pattern
at top corners of
back and front and
cut away as diagram

Top
**ARM-
HOLE**

NIGHTCAP

Back

Cut two

Fold

25cm

30cm   12in

Slit
back

Side edge   Side edge

SKIRT

10in

LOUISA'S AND EMILY'S NIGHTGOWN AND NIGHTCAP:
WINTER AND SUMMER VERSIONS

5. Bind the edge of each sleeve. Stitch lace to overlap the lower edge, sewing the top edge of the lace close against the folded edge of the binding (take care to leave a wide enough channel for the elastic). Stitch another row of lace, just above the top edge of the binding, to fall over the previous row. Thread 11cm (4¼in) elastic through the binding and draw up to fit the arms.

6. Fit garment on doll and turn up the hem. Thread 1.5mm (¹⁄₁₆in) ribbon through the lace, then sew around the hem, about 2cm (¾in) above the lower edge.

7. Catch 6mm (¼in) ribbon across the front, over the waistline gathers. Make a rose from 3mm (⅛in) ribbon (see chapter 2). Fold a 30cm (12in) length of ribbon in half for the streamers, stitch behind the rose, then stitch to centre front of waistline.

8. Cut the nightcap brim in interlining, slightly smaller, as broken line on pattern. Tack to the wrong side of one brim piece. Right sides together, stitch the two brim pieces together around the outer edge, just beyond the interlining, leaving the straight back edge open. Trim close to the seam with pinking shears, then turn to the right side. Top-stitch neatly, close to the seam. Tack along the back edge, and mark into eight, as notches.

9. Join the two back pieces along the straight edge. Turn to the right side and gather close to this edge, but don't draw up. Tack the two pieces together all round the outer edge. Mark the edge into eight, as notches. Gather all round the curved edge.

10. Pin the brim and back together, matching the marked points: draw up to fit and stitch, distributing the gathers evenly between the pins.

11. Fit the cap on the doll and draw up the back gathers to fit, about 6cm (2½in).

12. Mark the outer edge of the brim into eight, as notches. Mark the nightcap lace into eight, then gather. Pin the straight edge just inside the brim, matching notches; draw up to fit and stitch, distributing the gathers evenly between the pins.

13. Cut two 15cm (6in) lengths of 1.5mm (¹⁄₁₆in) wide ribbon: stitch inside the brim at crosses for ties.

EMILY'S WARM WINTER NIGHTGOWN AND MATCHING NIGHTCAP

Touches of black lace at collar, cuffs and hem add sophistication to a nightgown designed to keep a young lady cosy in the draughtiest bedroom. Emily's practical winter version of Louisa's frothy nightdress is in a warm red fabric dotted with clusters of tiny flowers. The matching nightcap keeps her ears warm too.

– MATERIALS –

40cm (½yd) cotton-type fabric, 90cm (36in) wide
6×23cm (2½×9in) heavy-weight non-woven interlining (Vilene or equivalent)
1.70m (2yd) black lace, 10mm (⅜in) deep
50cm (½yd) white lace, 10mm (⅜in) deep (for nightcap)
30cm (12in) satin ribbon, 1.5mm (¹⁄₁₆in) wide
70cm (¾yd) matching bias binding
25cm (¼yd) narrow round elastic
2 snap fasteners

1. Cut two pieces of fabric 30cm (12in) deep × 25cm (10in) wide for the skirt back and front. Trace the pattern for the armhole and cut away this section at the top corners of each fabric piece (see diagram). Cut the yoke front once: cut the yoke back and the (winter) sleeve, and the nightcap brim and back, twice each.

2. Make a 6cm (2½in) slit for the centre back opening (see line on diagram): bind both edges, then make a tiny pleat to neaten the base, turning one bound edge back to close over the other.

3. Mark the top edge of the skirt front equally into four, then gather. Right sides together, pin to the lower edge of the yoke front, matching marked points to notches: draw up to fit, distributing the gathers evenly, and stitch. Turn the seam up behind the yoke and top-stitch the lower edge of the yoke to hold in place.

4. Gather and join the skirt back to the back pieces of the yoke in the same way, but have the bound edge level with the broken line on the yoke pattern, allowing the remainder of the centre back to extend beyond. When the joining is complete, turn these edges back inside (as broken line), fold the raw edges neatly under and stitch for the centre back opening.

5. Join the shoulder seams.

6. Mark the centre at the top edge of each sleeve, then gather between the circles. Fit the sleeve into the armhole, matching side edges and notches, and centre top with the shoulder seam. Draw up the gathers to fit, distributing them evenly between the marked points, and stitch. Clip curves.

7. Join the side seams of the sleeve and skirt.

8. Bind the neck edge. Mark 23cm (9in) lace into four, then gather and pin around the neckline, the marked points at centre front and shoulders, the top edge of the lace close against the lower edge of the binding: draw up to fit, and stitch neatly. Repeat with another 23cm (9in) length of lace, this time pinning it to the upper (folded) edge of the binding: draw up and oversew into place.

9. Bind the edge of each sleeve. Stitch lace to overlap the lower edge, sewing the top edge of the lace close against the folded edge of the binding (take care to leave a wide enough channel for the elastic). Stitch another row of lace, just above the top edge of the binding, to fall over the previous row. Thread 10cm (4in) elastic through the binding and draw up to fit wrists.

10. Stitch snap fasteners to the yoke for the centre back opening.

11. Fit garment on doll and turn up the hem. Stitch lace level with the lower edge.

12. Follow the directions for Louisa's Matching Nightcap (above: steps 8–13).

CHAPTER 12

WILLIAM, THE GREENAWAY GIRLS' HOUND

*T*he great love in the girls' lives is small and round and very cuddly: he has the most affectionate nature, and adores his four mistresses just as much as they love him. He's shamefully spoilt, very *mischievous* and just a little bit vain – but is it really surprising?

WILLIAM

*I*f you can make a pompon, you can make William. Use a bouclé-type yarn to achieve that lovely curly coat, but any ordinary medium-weight yarn will do if you can't find something crinkly.

– MATERIALS –

Putty-coloured knitting yarn, at least 28g
   (1oz): either crinkly, bouclé-type, or 4-ply/
   double-knit
8×13cm (3¼×5in) mid-brown felt
5cm (2in) square dark brown felt
Scrap of black felt
Light/medium-weight card
Polyester stuffing (or wadding or cotton wool)
Strong thread or fine string
10cm (4in) single-face satin ribbon, 6mm
   (¼in) wide
50cm (½yd) satin ribbon, 3mm (⅛in) wide
Large tapestry needle
Clear adhesive

– TO MAKE A POMPON: –

Cut two card circles as pattern. Fold a 4m (4yd) length of yarn into four and thread into a tapestry needle (have fewer strands if the yarn is thicker). Wrap the yarn evenly over and over the two card circles (as diagram A): continue going round and round, until the central hole is completely filled (diagram B).

Push pointed scissors through the yarn and *between* the two card circles (arrow on diagram B): cut the yarn all the way round (keeping scissors between the card). Slip a piece of strong thread or fine string between the two layers of card to surround the yarn in the centre: knot together, pulling as tight as you can. Cut away the card, then trim the pompon severely to make a neat, round, firm ball.

1. Make two pompons for the body and one for the head: reserve 2m (2yd) yarn for finishing – you can use all the remaining yarn if necessary.

2. Slightly flatten one side of each of the body pompons, then glue firmly together, pushing them close into each other. Glue the head into position, as illustrated.

3. To make the feet, cut four soles in card: glue these to dark brown felt and cut the felt 2mm (¹⁄₁₆in) larger all round,

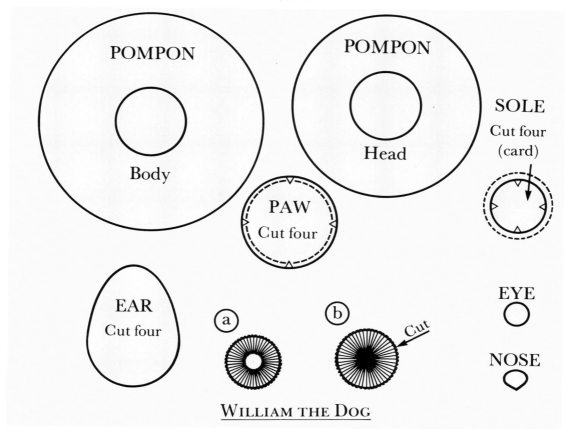

POMPON
Body

POMPON
Head

SOLE
Cut four
(card)

PAW
Cut four

EAR
Cut four

ⓐ

ⓑ

Cut

EYE

NOSE

WILLIAM THE DOG

as broken line. Cut four paws in mid-brown felt. Mark notches and gather all round the edge of each paw, with very tiny stitches as indicated, then pin to the sole (card inside), matching notches. Draw up the gathers to fit and oversew neatly three-quarters of the way round: push a little stuffing inside, then complete stitching. Glue the feet under the body, as illustrated.

4. Wind 1m (1yd) yarn round the tip of your forefinger: remove and catch together to form a bunch of loops. Glue this, end down, inside the top of the head to form his top-knot, as illustrated. Cut the loops and trim neatly.

5. Twist eight 10cm (4in) lengths of yarn tightly together: fold in half to form a twisted cord, and bind the ends neatly with thread. Trim the end, then glue

down inside the back of the body for his tail.

6. Cut the ear four times in mid-brown felt. Oversew one pair together all round for each ear, then glue to the head as illustrated.

7. Cut the eyes and nose in black felt and glue to the face, as shown.

8. Make a bow (method B in chapter 2) from 8cm (3in) of 6mm (¼in) ribbon and glue below the top-knot.

9. Cut a length of 3mm (⅛in) ribbon for his collar and glue the ends together around the neck. Pass one end of the remaining ribbon through the collar, for the lead, and glue the loop: glue the other end back to form a loop to hold the lead.

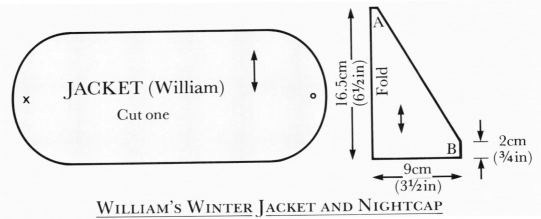

JACKET (William)

Cut one

×   ○

A

16.5cm
(6½in)

Fold

B

2cm
(¾in)

9cm
(3½in)

WILLIAM'S WINTER JACKET AND NIGHTCAP

WILLIAM'S WINTER JACKET

*W*illiam won't go out without his smart little coat when there's frost in the air or snow on the ground. Edge it with very narrow braid, either plaited from ribbon (see chapter 2) or, as shown here, a wider braid cut in half. The same braid – full-width – is used here for the strap under his tummy.

– MATERIALS –

5×9cm (2×3½in) light-weight woollen fabric
25cm (10in) very narrow braid
7cm (3in) matching braid, about 6–10mm (¼–⅜in) wide
Snap fastener
Clear adhesive

———————— . ————————

1. Cut the pattern once in fabric.

2. Glue very narrow braid all round, just overlapping the cut edge.

3. Sew one end of the wider braid under one side of the jacket at the cross. Measure the braid under his tummy and cut it to length. Stitch the snap fastener on the other side, at the circle.

WILLIAM'S NIGHTCAP

*W*illiam has had such a busy day that he's so tired he can hardly keep his eyes open. But even so, he always sleeps better with his nightcap on – perhaps it helps to keep his thoughts together.

– MATERIALS –

18×20cm (7×8in) striped medium-weight cotton-type fabric
Scrap of white knitting yarn
Scrap of stiff card
Pipe cleaner or chenille stem (optional)

———————— . ————————

1. Draw your pattern following the diagram, and cut in fabric.

2. Join the centre back seam between A and B. Make a 1cm (⅜in) hem around the lower edge. Turn to the right side.

3. Make a tassel as described for Emily's Tasselled Purse (chapter 8), winding the yarn 15–20 times (according to thickness) around a 2.5cm (1in) deep piece of card. Stitch it to the point of the cap.

4. In order to bend the cap round and hold it in the required position, a pipe cleaner may be inserted: push one end into the point of the cap and stitch the other end at the base of the seam.

CHAPTER 13

THE GREENAWAY GIRLS' FURNITURE

The elegant furniture in the Greenaway household is all made from throwaway cartons and boxes. Empty grocery cartons provide the rigid corrugated card that forms the basic construction: medium-weight card comes from good-quality cereal packets (the leading brands are usually packed in the best quality card!), whilst light-weight card can be found in crispbread packets. The footstool is made of rolled-up scrap paper, and the table stands on an empty salt container (though you can use rolled-up paper for this too, if you're on a salt-free diet!). A leftover length of wallpaper gives the wardrobe a professional finish.

When you've re-cycled your waste paper and card into the basic construction, add some spectacular cover-ups in the form of luxuriously padded upholstery and pretty drapes, all trimmed with silk fringe and satin ribbons.

Pick up plenty of empty cartons from the checkout of your local supermarket, or ask your grocer or off-licence for a supply of suitable ones (wine and spirit bottles are usually packed in very good-quality boxes). Choose those made from firm, rigid, corrugated card, which has not been damaged or flattened. Avoid ones which are soft and bend easily, or any which have been stained or retain the smell of their contents. You will soon discover how to discriminate.

Then cut the pieces for your furniture from the most suitable areas. It is usually best to have the ridges in the corrugated card going vertically, and this is indicated by arrows on the patterns and diagrams.

Take care to cut the pieces very accurately, using a sharp craft knife and a metal rule, or they won't fit together properly. Score, where indicated, with a blunt table knife.

You can, of course, use any fabric to upholster the chair and footstool, so long as it is not too thick: but the ones illustrated are covered with 'babycord', which is the finest kind of needlecord, and looks almost like a luxury velvet. It is easy to use, and very effective. The rest of the furniture is covered with firmly woven cotton-type dress fabrics in a variety of pretty prints, and the drapes are plain voile sheer curtain net. Plan an attractive colour scheme before you begin. The girls chose pink and blue and white, as you can see from the pictures of them in their home.

The trimmings shown are a mixture of furnishing and lampshade braids, silky lampshade fringe and braid plaited in toning colours from satin ribbon (see chapter 2). Plaited ribbon braid is ideal for this purpose: it allows you to mix and match your fabrics in lots of exciting ways, and it enhances the furniture because it is obviously custom-made. Study the illustrations to see the way the braid is carefully designed to complete each item.

Note: See the Guidelines in chapter 2 for more advice about working with the above materials, and the recommended tools to use.

Making Cylindrical Bases for the Furniture

1. Find a piece of fairly thin card (cereal or crispbread packet) which is at least 2.5cm (1in) larger all round than the diameter of the cylinder you are planning to make. Cut a circle in the centre of the card, exactly the diameter of the cylinder you require.

2. Cut a lot of strips of smooth, flat, cartridge/wallpaper-weight scrap paper: pages from good-quality magazines and catalogues will do, but the larger the cylinder the stiffer the paper you will need. Each strip should be the depth of your cylinder and *at least* 30cm (12in) long.

3. Roll up one strip of paper, place it inside the circle and allow it to open out so that it fits snugly against the cut edge of the hole: remove, and glue the overlap.

4. Roll up another strip of paper and repeat inside the cylinder made by the first strip, edge to edge with the previous strip: make sure the top and bottom edges are exactly level. Lightly glue the new strip to the last one to hold it in place.

5. Continue – adding several sheets at a time – until you have built up a firm, strong shell. It doesn't matter how much paper you roll up inside – it all adds valuable weight to make your base solid and steady.

Birthday Breakfast Table and Stools

*T*he combination of Wedgwood blue and *crisp white is fresh as the morning for this charming breakfast set, designed to set off the delicate wild strawberry Wedgwood china. Comfortable stools are just the right height for the dolls to sit at table to enjoy a*

refreshing cup of coffee while Louisa opens her birthday presents.

The set of furniture illustrated in chapter 5 is made from five empty table salt canisters: but don't despair if you don't eat salt, and can't find any other canister with similar dimensions. Simply make your own cylinders as described above.

– Materials –

5 cylinders, 14.5cm (5¾in) high × 8cm (3in) in diameter
Corrugated cardboard
Medium-weight card
White covering paper
Coloured covering paper to match fabric (optional)
50cm (⅝yd) blue medium-weight cotton-type fabric, 90cm (36in) wide
30cm (12in) square similar fabric in white
25cm (10in) square medium-weight polyester wadding
2.20m (2½yd) satin ribbon, 1.5mm (¹⁄₁₆in) wide
OR 60cm (¾yd) very narrow matching braid
1.30m (1½yd) narrow white lace
Adhesive tape
Dry stick adhesive (optional)
Clear adhesive

---

1. For the table base, use three salt canisters or make three cylinders as directed above to the required dimensions. Place the three cylinders together as figure a and tape right round them at the top and bottom to hold firmly in position. (If using salt canisters, keep the lids on: but if you have made your own cylinders, don't worry about not having a 'top'.) Wrap coloured or white paper round the three cylinders and glue the join, trimming level at top and bottom.

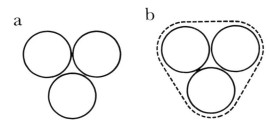

a   b

2. Spread glue liberally over the top edges (or lids) of the cylinders, then turn upside down and press down firmly on a piece of card. When dry, trim the card as broken line on figure b.

3. Cut two 20cm (8in) diameter circles in card. Glue each to a piece of corrugated board: trim the corrugated board level with the circle. Then glue the two circles together, *corrugated inside* (have the ridges running in opposite directions at right angles). Glue a sheet of white paper over the top side of the table and trim it level with the edge. (This is only necessary if you are planning a white tablecloth – to avoid the buff colour of the card showing through.)

4. Cut a strip of blue fabric 18cm (7in) deep × 90cm (36in) wide for the skirt. Join the two short edges and press the seam open. Mark the top edge equally into eight, then gather quite close to the edge. Mark the top edge of the table into eight (with a pencil – erase later), then pin the skirt round, matching the marked points and pushing pins between the layers of corrugated cardboard. Draw up to fit round the cut edge of the table top, distributing the gathers evenly and adding more pins to hold in place temporarily. Then, section by section, glue the gathered edge to the table top.

5. Fit the table top on the base and turn up the hem. Remove and stitch. Press the hem, then lower the skirt over the base and glue the table top firmly down onto it.

6. Cut a 30cm (12in) square of white fabric for the cloth: trim the edges absolutely straight, following the woven thread. Stitch lace so that it just overlaps the edge, taking care to turn the corners very neatly.

7. To make each stool, either cut down a canister to measure 11cm (4¼in): or make a cylinder 8cm (3in) in diameter × 11cm (4in) high. Cover with coloured or white paper.

8. Cut a strip of blue fabric 13cm (5¼in) deep × 45cm (18in) wide for the skirt. Join the two short edges and press the seam open. Mark the top edge equally into eight, then gather 1cm (⅜in) below the edge. Mark the top edge of the cylinder into eight, then pin the skirt round, matching the marked points. Draw up the gathers to fit around the top of the cylinder, then turn the overlapping fabric over the edge and glue down inside. Turn up the hem and stitch.

9. Cut two 8cm (3in) diameter circles of card for the seat. Glue each to a piece of corrugated board: trim the corrugated board level with the card circles. Glue the circles together, as for the table top (step 3). Cut two 8cm (3in) circles of wadding and glue lightly to the top side of the seat.

10. Cut a 14cm (5½in) diameter circle of blue fabric. Gather all round the edge, then place the circle right-side down and rest the seat in the centre, wadding side down: draw up the gathers tightly underneath the seat, so it is smoothly covered. Glue on top of the base.

11. Plait three 36cm (15in) lengths of ribbon to make braid (as chapter 2): glue on top of the skirt gathers.

VELVET UPHOLSTERED CHAIR

*L*uxuriously padded and upholstered in velvet-look 'babycord', it's hard to believe that this charming little chair (chapters 5 and 6) is made from old cartons and a cornflakes packet! It looks lovely in dusky rose pink, trimmed with matching braid made from plaited satin ribbon in exactly the same shade. But you probably have very different ideas. You might choose vivid blue, rich ruby or deep purple: in each

case you could match the colour for your trimming or design a dramatic contrast. They would all look wonderful. And when you've made the chair, don't forget a soft cushion and matching footstool to complete the comfortable picture.

– MATERIALS –

Corrugated cardboard
Medium-weight card
35×60cm (14×24in) babycord (or similar fabric)
20×60cm (8×24in) medium-weight wadding
40cm (½yd) silky lampshade fringe, 25mm (1in) deep (plain top edge)
5.50m (6yd) satin ribbon, 1.5mm (¹⁄₁₆in) wide
Clear adhesive

———— · ————

1. Draw out your pattern for the back on 1cm (³⁄₈in) squared paper, following the pattern diagram: draw a 14cm (5¼in) diameter circle (centre A), with a 10× 11cm (3¾×4⅛in) box 4cm (1½in) below it (C–C–D–D), then join points B–C at each side. Draw the base pattern as shown.

2. Cut these two pieces and the seat from medium-weight card. Score the broken lines on the base and seat.

3. Bend the base round and glue the tabs *behind* the lower section of the chair back (matching points C–D). Bend down the back section of the seat and glue inside the base of the back (matching points C–C). Cut a separate piece of corrugated board to fit inside each side of the base and glue it into position. Then cut several more pieces to fit inside the front only, and glue these one behind another: this is to build up the weight at the front, so make the front section at least 2.5cm (1in) thick. Glue the seat down over the base.

4. Cut a strip of fabric 12cm (4½in) deep × 40cm (15in) wide for the skirt (fray the bottom edge to make sure it is absolutely straight). Gather the top edge.

Glue the side edges behind the back (over the base tabs), then draw up the gathers to fit the seat, distributing them evenly and gluing around the edge of the seat so that the bottom edge just touches the ground.

5. Cut the back again, this time in corrugated cardboard. Place this on the wrong side of your babycord and cut the fabric 1.5cm (½in) larger all round except the lower edge D–D, which should be cut level. Snip the surplus at the widest point on each side, then bring the surplus at each side below the snips up and over, gluing it smoothly to the card. Cut the surplus all round the top into small tabs, then glue them smoothly to the card in the same way. Glue this piece behind the back of the chair.

6. Cut the back once more in corrugated board, but omit the base section below C–C: then cut off 5mm (³⁄₁₆in) above C–C. Cut the seat also, omitting the section above C–C. Cut two layers of wadding the same size as this seat piece and glue lightly on top. Place the seat, wadding down, on the wrong side of the babycord (direction of fabric from back to front), and cut the fabric 2cm (¾in) larger all round. Fold the surplus fabric over the straight edge and glue. Then gather all round the curved edge: draw up the gathers to fit, and either sew or stick each corner, distributing the gathers evenly between.

7. Pad and cover the back section in exactly the same way. Glue the back section into place, followed by the seat.

8. Glue fringe around the skirt, bottom edges level. Make appropriate lengths of plaited ribbon (as chapter 2) and glue into place as follows: around the edge of the seat; around the back, ending where it meets the seat trim: across the base of the back; and over the top edge of the fringe.

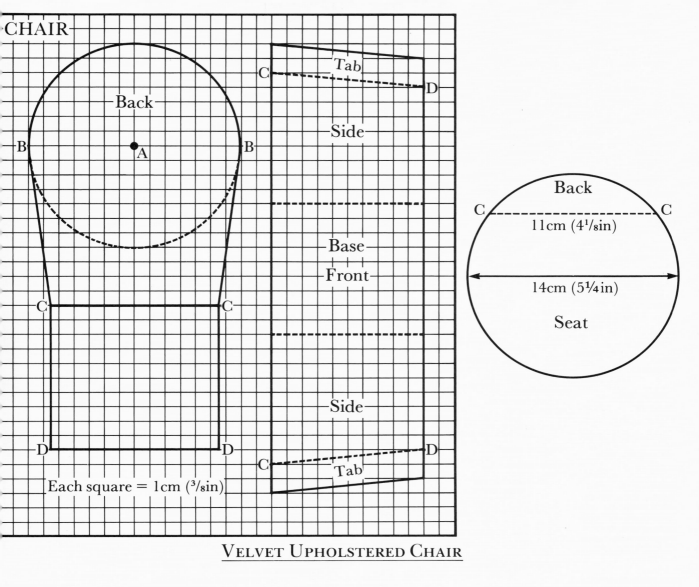

CHAIR

Back

A

B · · B

C —— C

D —— D

Each square = 1cm (³⁄₈in)

Tab

C · · · · D

Side

Base

Front

Side

C · · · · D

Tab

Back

C - - - - - - C

11cm (4¹⁄₈in)

14cm (5¹⁄₄in)

Seat

VELVET UPHOLSTERED CHAIR

CUSHION

Cut two

Place fold in tracing paper against line

ROUND CUSHION

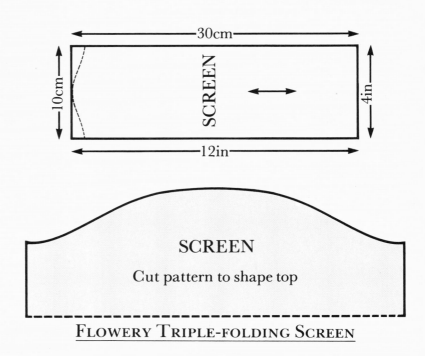

30cm

10cm

SCREEN

4in

12in

SCREEN

Cut pattern to shape top

FLOWERY TRIPLE-FOLDING SCREEN

Matching Padded Footstool

– Materials –

Thin card
Medium-weight card
Medium-weight scrap paper
15×25cm (6×10in) babycord (or similar fabric)
15×30cm (6×12in) medium-weight wadding
1.50m (1¾yd) satin ribbon, 1.5mm (¹⁄₁₆in wide
Clear adhesive

———— · ————

1. Cut a 6cm (2½in) diameter circle in the centre of a piece of thin card. Cut quite a lot of 3cm (1¼in) wide strips of paper, about 30cm (12in) long. Roll up one strip of paper, fit it inside the circle and allow it to open out so it fits snugly against the cut edge of the hole: remove and glue the overlap. Roll up another strip of paper and repeat inside the cylinder made with the first strip: glue the ends to hold in place. Continue until you have built up a firm shell, then add the remaining strips, several at a time, to fill the circle.

2. Cover the outside of the cylinder with two layers of wadding, cutting them level with the edges. Cut a strip of babycord fabric 6cm (2½in) deep × 23cm (9in) wide: wrap round over the wadding, overlapping both edges equally, and glue the join neatly. Cut the surplus into small tabs, then take them neatly over the edge and glue them down over the rolled paper.

3. Cut two 6cm (2½in) diameter circles of medium-weight card. Cut an 8cm(3in) diameter circle of babycord and gather round the edge: glue a card circle lightly to the wrong side of the fabric, then draw up the gathers evenly all round and secure. Cover the second card circle with 3–4 layers of wadding, making the *final* layer 5mm (¼in) larger all round.

Cut a 10cm (4in) circle of babycord, gather the edge, place the padded circle in the centre (wadding to wrong side of fabric), and draw up tightly underneath. Glue the circles to the top and bottom of the footstool.

4. Plait the ribbon to make two lengths of braid (see chapter 2), and glue over the joins at top and bottom.

Round Cushion

– Materials –

Two 9cm (3½in) diameter circles of medium-weight cotton-type flowered fabric
30cm (12in) *flat* lace, 10mm (³⁄₈in) deep (*note*: only use flat lace if it will follow curved edge)
OR 50cm (½yd) lace, if it needs to be gathered
1.50m (1½yd) satin ribbon, 1.5mm (¹⁄₁₆in) wide
Polyester stuffing (or wadding snipped into tiny pieces)
Clear adhesive

———— · ————

1. Cut the pattern twice in fabric.

2. Right sides together, join round the edge, leaving open between the notches: turn back the raw edges and tack. Clip seam (with pinking shears, if possible), and turn to the right side.

3. Top-stitch neatly very close to the seam to make a firm edge and emphasise the shape. Stuff lightly and close the seam.

4. Stitch lace (flat or gathered) around the edge. Plait the ribbon to make braid (as chapter 2), and glue over the lower edge of the lace.

SMALL SIDE TABLE WITH FRINGED CLOTH

*T*his is a useful little table which can be dressed up in lots of different guises: other versions are illustrated in chapters 6 and 8, 4 and 11. This one is based on a salt canister, but any similar card or plastic container would do, cut down to size if necessary, or you could make your own cylinder as described above. The height is 14.5cm (5¾in), but the diameter is unimportant, as long as it is wide enough to stand firmly.

– MATERIALS –

Cylindrical base, 14.5cm (5¾in) high
Corrugated cardboard
Medium-weight card
Medium-weight covering paper
25cm (10in) medium-weight cotton-type fabric, 90cm (36in) wide
1m (1yd) silky lampshade fringe, 25mm (1in) deep
Dry stick adhesive (optional)
Clear adhesive

———— · ————

1. Cover the cylinder with plain or coloured paper.

2. Cut a piece of fabric 60cm (24in) wide × 17.5cm (7in) deep – or 3cm (1¼in) more than the height of your cylinder – for the skirt. Join the short edges, then mark the top edge into eight and make two rows of gathers, 3–4mm (⅛in) apart.

3. Cut two 12cm (5in) diameter circles of card: glue each to corrugated board and cut the board level with the card circles. Rule four lines across the centre of one to divide it into eight equal sections, then pin the skirt gathers round the edge, matching the marked points and drawing them up to fit evenly: glue the surplus fabric above the gathers down over the edge of the card circle, and remove the pins.

4. Cover the second card circle with paper, then glue it on top of the first one.

5. Glue the cylinder firmly underneath the circles and leave to dry.

6. Turn up the hem of the skirt and stitch.

7. Cut the tablecloth 22cm (8½in) square and stitch fringe all round the edge. Drape over the table as illustrated.

FLOWERY TRIPLE-FOLDING SCREEN

*D*epending on the thickness of your fabric, you may find it a good idea to create an extra smooth surface by covering both sides of the screen with thin card before pasting on the covering fabric. (Illustrated in chapter 6.)

– MATERIALS –

Corrugated cardboard
Small piece of thin card
35×70cm (14×28in) flowered medium-weight cotton-type fabric
60cm (¾yd) single-face matching satin ribbon, about 16mm (⅝in) wide (optional)
14m (16yd) satin ribbon, 1.5mm (1/16in) wide
1m (1⅛yd) furnishing braid, 10mm (⅜in) wide
60cm (¾yd) cotton tape, 10–15mm (½in) wide
Wallpaper (or similar) paste
Clear adhesive

———— · ————

1. Cut nine 30×10cm (12×4in) pieces from corrugated cardboard (direction of ridges as arrow on pattern diagram). Trace the pattern and make a card template to shape the top of each panel as broken line on diagram. Glue the pieces together to make three triple-thickness panels.

2. Place two panels side by side, the lower edges exactly level, and glue a length of tape down the centre to join them, forming a hinge. *Turn this section over* and join the third piece in the same way. Fold back each join with the tape inside, and glue ribbon (or a strip of fabric) neatly over the two cut edges.

3. Paste fabric smoothly over both sides of the screen, covering a double and a single panel on each side: trim the edges level when dry. Place under a board with some heavy books on top to ensure that the card dries absolutely flat.

4. Glue furnishing braid over each side edge and along the top of each panel.

5. Plait eight 30cm (12in) lengths of braid from narrow ribbon (see chapter 2) and glue four on each side of the screen: one over the cut edge of the fabric at each side of the ribbon-covered hinged fold; and two quite close together, on each side of the fabric-covered hinged fold. Make more plaited braid to glue over the cut edge of the fabric at the base of each panel.

FAIRYTALE RIBBON AND ROSES FOUR-POSTER BED

A bed fit for a princess to dream away the night. It isn't surprising that Louisa doesn't want to get up – even though it's her birthday (see chapter 4). Don't be misled into thinking that Louisa's bed is difficult to make just because it looks so spectacular. Throwaway grocery cartons and cereal packets form the structure, and the rest of the romantic illusion is created with pretty fabric (a tiny blue spot on a white ground), sheer curtain voile, embroidered ribbon and lots of delicate lace. It's worth shopping around for lace – you don't have to pay a lot: this one came from a local shop and was very inexpensive. Investigate small haberdashery shops, market stalls and stores which specialise in sari fabrics and trimmings. The width of lace illustrated does add the ultimate touch of luxury, but if you aren't lucky enough to find anything inexpensive in this width, just substitute a narrower one – your bed will still look as if it has escaped from a fairy story!

– MATERIALS –

Corrugated cardboard
Medium–weight card
Medium-weight white covering paper
Four 40cm (16in) lengths of wooden dowelling, 10mm (⅜in) diameter
Balsa wood, 3mm (⅛in) thick (see step 9)
1.30m (1½yd) medium-weight cotton-type fabric, 90cm (36in) wide, for the bed
90cm (1yd) sheer voile curtain net, 90cm (36in) wide
30×70cm (12×27in) light-weight lawn-type fabric, for the sheet and pillows
10m (11yd) white lace, preferably 30mm (1–1¼in) deep
3.70m (4¼yd) floral Jacquard ribbon, 16mm (⅝in) wide
1.40m (1½yd) single-face white satin ribbon, 10mm (⅜in) wide
1.70m (2yd) single-face Antique Blue satin ribbon, 10mm (⅜in) wide, for the roses
1.20m (1⅜yd) Antique Blue feather-edge satin ribbon, 10mm (⅜in) wide
4m (4yd) Willow (green) satin ribbon, 1.5mm (1/16in) wide
Thick and/or medium-weight polyester wadding (for amount, see steps 5, 16, 20 and 21)
Polyester stuffing (or use wadding) (see steps 20 and 21)
Sandpaper
White enamel paint (plus undercoat, if necessary)
Tiny pins, approximately 15mm (⅝in) long
Adhesive tape
Latex adhesive (optional)
Wallpaper (or similar) paste (optional)
Dry stick adhesive
Clear adhesive

———— · ————

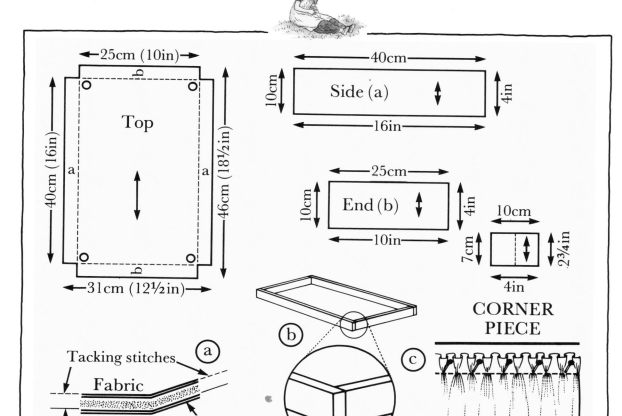

Diagram labels

Top — 25cm (10in); 40cm (16in); 46cm (18½in); 31cm (12½in); a; a; b; b

Side (a) — 40cm; 10cm; 16in; 4in

End (b) — 25cm; 10cm; 10in; 4in

Corner piece — 10cm; 7cm; 4in; 2¾in

Tacking stitches

Fabric

Edge of fabric

Ribbon

a b c

CORNER PIECE

FAIRYTALE RIBBON AND ROSES FOUR-POSTER BED

1. Cut the top of the base, two sides and two ends from corrugated board (as pattern diagram). Score the broken lines and bend tabs *a* and *b* down. Glue tabs *a* behind the sides, and tabs *b* behind the ends. Cut four small corner pieces of board as pattern diagram: score the broken lines and bend at right angles. Fit one inside each corner, below the tabs, to join the sides and ends: trim the lower edge level before gluing in place. Cut a strip of board to fit inside each side and end, between the corner pieces and below the tabs: glue in place.

2. Cut four 40cm (16in) lengths of dowelling for the posts. Make a small hole at each corner of the top of the base (at circles) and push the posts through: glue inside each inside corner of the base,

bottom of dowelling level with lower edge (tape across the base to hold in place). Cut strips of board to fit inside each side and end, between the posts and level with the top and bottom: glue into place. Paint the posts white and leave to dry.

3. Measure the exact size of the top of the base (allowing for thickness of sides and ends) and cut a piece of board this size (make a note of these measurements to cut the canopy later). Cut away each corner to fit round the posts, and glue to the top of the base.

4. Paste white paper smoothly over the top of the base, overlapping the sides and ends about 4cm (1½in), then cover the sides and ends in the same way.

5. Cut one or more layers of wadding the same size as the base, and glue lightly on top (tack together if more than one layer).

6. Cut a piece of fabric the size of the base *plus* 1cm (³⁄₈in) extra all round. Make a line of tacking all round, 1cm (³⁄₈in) from the edge, to indicate the edge of the bed. Pin the wrong side of the ribbon to the right side of the fabric, so top edge of ribbon is level with the marked line, and the lower edge overlaps the outer edge of the fabric, turning the corners neatly and accurately at a right angle (diagram (a)): stitch along the top edge of the ribbon. Make a small diagonal slit at each corner for the posts, then slip the fabric down over the base to check that it fits correctly.

7. Cut two 12×90cm (5×36in) strips across the fabric for the valance. Join the short side edges to form one big circle. Mark the top edge of each strip equally into eight, then gather. Mark with a pin the centre of the ribbon along each short edge of the top piece (head and foot of bed): then mark each side of the ribbon between the pins into eight. Pin the top edge of the valance behind the lower edge of the ribbon, with the joins at the centre of the head and foot (your first two pins), and matching the marked points: draw up the gathers to fit, distributing them evenly, and stitch the lower edge of the ribbon over the gathering line. Fit over the bed to measure length, then remove to turn up and stitch the hem. Sew lace all round the bottom, lower edges of lace and valance level. Fit back over the bed.

8. Cut a piece of corrugated cardboard, the same size as the top of the bed, for the canopy. Cut two pieces of card the same size: cover the plain side of each of these with white paper (dry stick adhesive may be used for this, but paste is less extravagant). When dry, glue one piece of card to each side of the

corrugated board: place under a tray or board weighted with books to ensure that it dries absolutely flat. When dry, cover the underside with fabric, trimming level with the edge (this step may be omitted if using a dark or otherwise unsuitable fabric): use dry stick adhesive for preference, otherwise paste.

9. Cut two strips of balsa wood 2cm (³⁄₄in) deep × the length of your bed. Cut two more strips the width of the bed *minus 6mm (¹⁄₄in)*. Glue and pin together, the short strips *between* the long ones, to form a rectangular frame (diagram (b)). Sandpaper smooth, then paint the inside and the lower edge. When quite dry, glue and then pin the fabric-covered underside of the canopy to the top edge of the frame.

10. Cut a piece of fabric the size of the top *plus 2cm (³⁄₄in) extra all round*. Place over the canopy, overlapping equally all round (pin to the balsa wood temporarily). Glue the overlap neatly down all round over the balsa frame, trimming and turning in neatly at the corners. Glue white satin ribbon all round, level with the lower edge of the frame, to cover raw edge of fabric.

11. Cut the curtain for the head of the bed in voile, 40cm (16in) deep × 90cm (36in) wide (draw threads to mark your cutting line, as it is essential to follow the line of the fabric in making up the curtains). Turn a narrow hem over to the *right side* along the side and lower edges. Stitch lace on top, covering the raw edge and overlapping the edge of the curtain: gather the lace tightly to turn the corners.

12. Fit the canopy over the bed and pin the top edge of the curtain flat round it, so that the edge of the lace just touches the floor. Very carefully draw a thread level with the top edge of the white ribbon surrounding the canopy. Draw

another thread 6–7mm (¼in) above the first one. Remove the curtain from the bed. Gather along the *lower* thread line, but don't draw up. Then cut away the excess at the top along the upper thread line.

13. Mark the top edge of the curtain equally into eight. Mark the head end of the canopy frame into four. Then mark 5 and 10cm (2 and 4in) from the top corner at each side of the canopy. Pin the curtain round the head of the bed, matching the marked points, by pushing tiny pins in at a slanting angle, so that they penetrate the wood but do not go through it: don't push the pins all the way in, but position them so that the protruding top section is almost flat against the frame. Draw up the gathers to fit, then continue pinning between the existing pins, at 1cm (⅜in) intervals, distributing the gathers evenly as you go (diagram (c)).

14. Cut two curtains for the end of the bed, each 40×30cm (16×12in). Prepare as for the head of the bed, then position the centre of each curtain at the corner, drawing up the gathers to cover 6cm (2¼in) at each side.

15. Measure all round the edge of the canopy, over the curtain gathers, and add 1cm (⅜in) overlap – approximately 138cm (54½in). Cut embroidered ribbon this length and stitch top edge of lace along the lower edge, so that the lace overlaps below. Glue ribbon around the centre of the frame, over the curtain gathers. ·

16. For the coverlet, cut a piece of fabric 62cm (25in) long × the width of the bed *plus* 2cm (¾in). Fold in half to measure 31cm (12½in) long, and mark the fold line (this will be the top edge). Cut a piece of wadding 30cm (12in) long × the width of your bed. Tack this to the wrong side of one half of the fabric, level with the fold line and with 1cm (½in)

surplus fabric round the edges. Fold the fabric along the fold line, right side inside, and join the sides and bottom, leaving 10cm (4in) open at the centre of the bottom edge. Trim the seams and corners, then turn to the right side: turn the raw edges inside and slip-stitch the opening.

17. Pin the top edge of the Jacquard ribbon around the sides and bottom of the coverlet, overlapping 1cm (½in) at each end, and turning the corners neatly at a right angle. Oversew the ribbon to the edge of the coverlet, but leave 1cm (⅜in) unstitched at each side of the bottom corners: then turn under the free corners and catch underneath.

18. Cut two strips of fabric 9cm (3½in) deep × 70cm (27in) wide, for the sides: join the short edges to form one long strip. Gather the top edge, beginning and ending 1cm (⅜in) from the side edge. Pin round sides and bottom, behind the ribbon, as directed for the valance (step 7), then draw up to fit, distributing the gathers evenly, and stitch the lower edge of the ribbon over the gathering line. Turn up and stitch a 1cm (⅜in) hem, then hem the side edges neatly. Stitch lace all round, level with the lower edge.

19. Cut a 40cm (16in) square of fabric for the sheet. Turn under and stitch a very narrow double hem all round the edge. Trim the top edge of the sheet with lace.

20. For the pillow, cut a piece of fabric 22×18cm (8½×7in): fold in half to measure 11×18cm (4¼×7in) and mark the fold line. If using wadding, open out and tack several 10×16cm (3¾×6¼in) layers to the wrong side of one half of the fabric, level with the fold line and with 1cm (⅜in) surplus round the edges. Fold the fabric along the fold line, right side inside, and join the long edge and one

short end. Trim the seams and corners, then turn to the right side: turn the raw edges inside and slip-stitch the opening. If using stuffing, fold in half as indicated above, right side inside, and join the long edge and one short end. Trim the seams and corners and turn to the right side. Stuff fairly firmly, pushing well into the corners. Then turn the raw edges inside and slip-stitch the opening. Gather 1m (1yd) of lace and stitch round the edge, distributing the gathers evenly.

21. Make an under-pillow in the same way, but without the lace trimming.

22. To make each corner decoration, mark a 97cm (35in) length of Willow ribbon 1cm (½in) from one end, and then at 5cm (2in) intervals to the other end. Form into a looped rosette by bringing your needle and thread through the first marked point and then down through the second, up through the third and down through the next – all the way to the end, as if you were doing an elongated running stitch along the length of the ribbon. Draw up tightly and stitch through the centre to hold the shape, then secure the thread. Glue one at each top corner as illustrated, with a rose in the centre made from 30cm (12in) of 10mm (⅜in) Antique Blue ribbon (as method in chapter 2).

23. To tie back the curtains at the foot of the bed, loop a 10cm (4in) length of feather-edge ribbon around the curtain and post, and stitch a 1cm (⅜in) overlap. Make a bow (method B in chapter 2) from 20cm (8in) of the same ribbon, and stitch a rose in the centre made from 25cm (10in) of 10mm (⅜in) ribbon. Stitch the bow over the join in the loop.

ROSEBUD AND RIBBONS BEDROOM TABLE

*M*atching the bed and dressing table, the colour scheme and fabrics for this dainty little table give the same fairytale effect (see chapters 4 and 11). The blue teatable illustrated in chapters 6 and 8 is a slightly larger and simpler version of this design: the skirt and top are made in the same way, but there is no overskirt or lace trimming. A salt canister forms the basis of this one: but you can make a cylindrical base from scrap paper (as described above) if you can't find a suitable container.

– **MATERIALS** –

Cylindrical container, 14.5cm (5¾in) high
Corrugated cardboard
Medium-weight card
White covering paper
20cm (¼yd) medium-weight cotton-type fabric, 90cm (36in) wide (as the bed)
16×75cm (6¼×30in) sheer voile curtain net (as bed)
75cm (⅞yd) white lace, 30mm (1–1¼in) deep (as bed)
9cm (3½in) blue/white lace, 10mm (⅜in) deep
45cm (½yd) Antique Blue 'Fleur' woven satin ribbon, 10mm (⅜in) wide
1m (1yd) Antique Blue satin ribbon, 1.5mm (1/16in) wide
15cm (6in) Rosy Mauve single-face satin ribbon, 6mm (¼in) wide
Dry stick adhesive (optional)
Clear adhesive

———— · ————

1. Cover the cylinder with white paper.

2. Cut a piece of fabric 17.5cm (7in) deep × 60cm (24in) wide for the underskirt. Join the short edges, then mark the top into eight and make two rows of gathers, 3–4mm (⅛in) apart.

3. Cut a 12cm (5in) diameter circle of corrugated board. Rule four lines across the centre to divide it into eight equal

sections: then pin the skirt gathers round the edge, matching the marked points to the ends of the lines, and drawing them up to fit evenly. Glue the surplus fabric above the gathers down over the edge of the card circle, and remove the pins.

4. Join the short edges of the voile for the overskirt. Then gather and fix around the edge of another corrugated cardboard circle, as described in steps 2 and 3 for the underskirt.

5. Cut a third cardboard circle, then cover it first with card (plain side up), and then with white paper.

6. Slip the voile skirt down over the fabric one and glue the board circles firmly together.

7. Fit the skirts over the base and turn up the hem of the underskirt. Check the voile is 5mm (¼in) off the ground: trim if necessary. Remove and stitch the hem of the underskirt. Stitch lace around the lower edge of the overskirt, just touching the ground.

8. Cut a 16cm (6½in) circle of fabric for the table top. Gather all round the edge, then place the centre wrong side down on top of the third circle and draw up the gathers tightly underneath, so that the top is smoothly covered.

9. Glue the cylinder firmly under-neath the skirt circles, then glue the top over them. Leave to dry.

10. Glue 10mm (⅜in) ribbon all round the top edge, over the gathers.

11. Overlap and glue the cut ends of the narrow lace to form a circle. Gather the straight edge and draw up, leaving a small hole in the centre. Make a rose (as chapter 2) from the pink ribbon, and stitch it in the centre. Cut the very narrow ribbon into four, then fold in half and

catch behind the centre of the lace rosette. Stitch or glue to the side of the table, as illustrated.

ROSES AND LACE KIDNEY-SHAPED DRESSING TABLE

What could be more dreamily romantic than lacy drapes, a ruched skirt caught up with delicate pink roses round a kidney-shaped top and a mirror framed in pearls. There's a matching stool too – when a young lady wants to powder her nose (see chapter 11).

The dressing table is made from the same blue-spotted fabric and sheer white voile as the four-poster bed, and trimmed with the same lace. But as before, a narrower lace may be used instead. Materials for the stool and mirror are given separately below. Don't forget to add a fluffy pink powder-puff and giant pincushion!

– MATERIALS –

Corrugated cardboard
Medium-weight card
Medium-weight white covering paper
12×22cm (4¾×9in) stiff pale pink paper
20cm (¼yd) medium-weight cotton-type fabric, 90cm (36in) wide (as for the bed)
40cm (½yd) sheer voile curtain net, 90cm (36in) wide (as bed)
2.50m (2¾yd) white lace, preferably 30mm (1–1¼in) deep
45cm (½yd) blue/white lace, 10mm (⅜in) deep
70cm (¾yd) white single-face satin ribbon, 10mm (⅜in) wide
60cm (¾yd) Rosy Mauve single-face satin ribbon, 10mm (⅜in) wide
40cm (½yd) Rosy Mauve single-face satin ribbon, 6mm (¼in) wide
1.80m (2yd) Rosy Mauve satin ribbon, 1.5mm (¹⁄₁₆in) wide
30cm (12in) lampshade braid, 10mm (⅜in) wide
44cm (17½in) wooden dowelling, 5mm (³⁄₁₆in) in diameter
Balsa wood, 3mm (⅛in) thick (see step 13)

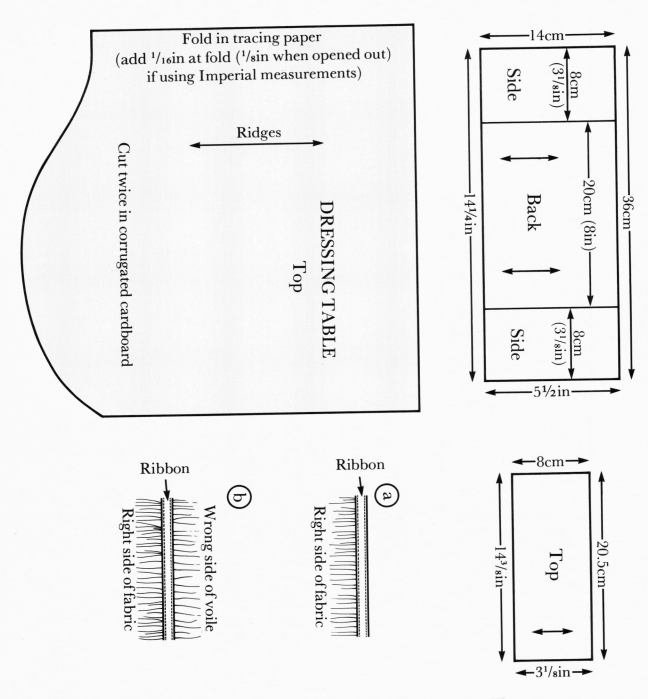

Fold in tracing paper
(add ¹/₁₆in at fold (¹/₈in when opened out)
if using Imperial measurements)

Ridges

Cut twice in corrugated cardboard

DRESSING TABLE

Top

14cm

8cm
(3¹/₈in)

Side

20cm (8in)

Back

8cm
(3¹/₈in)

Side

36cm

14¹/₄in

5½in

8cm

Top

14³/₈in

20.5cm

3¹/₈in

Ribbon

ⓑ

Right side of fabric

Wrong side of voile

Ribbon

ⓐ

Right side of fabric

ROSES AND LACE KIDNEY-SHAPED DRESSING TABLE

Sandpaper
White paint
Pins
Adhesive tape
Latex adhesive (optional)
Wallpaper (or similar) paste (optional)
Dry stick adhesive
Clear adhesive

———— · ————

1. Cut the back and sides in one piece, and the top, from corrugated cardboard according to the dimensions given.

2. Score the broken lines and bend the sides at right angles to the back. Fix the top temporarily in position with tape and pins: have the back edges level and any slight overlap equal on each side.

3. Cut a strip of card 6cm (2½in) wide × 20cm (8in) long, then score and fold in half lengthways: trim the length so that the strip fits across inside the angle between the back and the top. Glue into place so that the two pieces are securely joined. Repeat with strips of card 6×8cm (2½×3⅛in) to join the sides to the top.

4. Cut a piece of board to fit exactly inside the back, and glue it into place. Then glue pieces to reinforce the sides in the same way, and finally inside the top. This not only strengthens the construction, but adds weight.

5. Cover the whole of the inside smoothly with white covering paper, and also the sides and back on the outside. Glue braid down the front edges of the sides.

6. Trace your pattern for the shaped top (add ⅛in to the width if you are using imperial measurements): cut twice in corrugated cardboard and glue together. Cut again in card and glue on top (plain side up). Then cover with white paper. Finally, cover smoothly with pink paper. Glue on top of the base, back edges level, and overlapping at the sides and front.

7. Cut the skirt 16.5×90cm (6½×36in) across the width of your fabric. Make a double row of gathers 3mm (⅛in) apart along the top edge (it is easier to make two sets of gathers, divided at the centre). Mark the centre of your white ribbon: then mark each side of the ribbon 22cm (8¾in) from the centre. Mark each 22cm (8¾in) section equally into eight. Mark the top edge of your fabric into sixteen. Then, matching the marked points, pin the lower edge of the ribbon over the right side of the fabric, level with the bottom row of gathers (diagram (a)). Draw up the gathers, distributing them evenly between the pins, and stitch.

8. Cut a piece of voile 14×60cm (5½×25in) for the flounce. Turn under and stitch the short side edges. Gather the top edge, then join it to the other edge of the ribbon exactly as you did the skirt, but pin the ribbon over the *wrong* side of the voile (diagram (b)):

9. Mark the centre of the flounce and draw a vertical thread. Draw similar threads 11cm (4½in) each side of the centre. Then fold the flounce in half, wrong side inside, so that the lower edge is level with the ribbon: tack. Gather the double voile along each drawn thread, to 1cm (⅜in) from the top: draw up tightly and catch over the lower edge of the ribbon, where it joins the skirt. Repeat at each side edge. Top-stitch to hold the flounce down over the top edge of the ribbon. Finally, catch the bottom of each of the three centre sets of gathers to the skirt, and catch the side gathers to the selvedge of the skirt.

10. Fix the skirt to the front and sides of the shaped top by gluing the ribbon round the cut edge, centres matching and top edges level: *don't* glue the ends of the ribbon which extend beyond the skirt.

11. Plait three 60cm (24in) lengths of 1.5mm (¹⁄₁₆in) ribbon to make 45cm (18in) braid (as chapter 2), and glue it over the top edge of the flounce, level with the edge of the top.

12. Glue the shaped top securely to the top of the base. Glue the white ribbon ends across the back, overlapping at the centre.

13. Turn up and stitch the hem, then trim it with wide lace.

14. Rule a vertical line to mark the centre of the back of the base. Smooth the dowelling with sandpaper, then glue it over the marked line, the bottom level with the lower edge of the base. Cut four 14cm (5½in) strips of balsa wood 7–8mm (¼in) wide: glue one each side of the dowelling, fitting snugly against it, then glue the other two on top of the first ones. Paint all the wood white.

15. Cut a piece of voile 25×90cm (10×36in). Stitch lace along one long edge and both short ones, turning the corners neatly. Right side inside, fold in half to measure 25×45cm (10×18in), and draw a thread along the foldline. Join the two raw edges to form the centre back seam. Turn to the right side and make another line of stitches 1.5cm (½in) from the first one, beginning at the top fold and ending 15cm (6in) from the bottom. Gather along the centre top fold line, excluding the lace, and draw up very tightly. Slip the centre back channel down over the dowelling. Fix the drape at each back corner of the table.

16. To trim the front and sides, cut a 9cm (3½in) length of narrow lace: overlap and glue the cut ends to form a circle. Gather the straight edge and draw up, leaving a small hole in the centre. Make a rose (as chapter 2) from 20cm (8in) of 10mm (⅜in) ribbon and stitch in the centre of the lace rosette. Stitch over

the gathers, as illustrated. Make a similar trim, but use 15cm (6in) of lace to make a rosette with a 12–13mm (½in) hole in the centre: stitch a scrap of wide lace behind the centre of the rosette and trim away the excess. Make three tiny roses from 12cm (5in) of 6mm (¼in) ribbon and stitch them close together in the centre of the rosette. Stitch inside the centre top of the drape, as illustrated.

DRESSING TABLE STOOL

*T*he babycord used for the stool top is the same as that used to cover the upholstered chair (above). But any other medium-weight fabric would do as well, from velvet to a flower-printed cotton. Once again, a table salt canister was used for the base, but any similar container can be cut to size, or a cylindrical base can be made from scrap paper (as described above).

– MATERIALS –

Cylindrical container, 10cm (4in) high × 8cm (3¼in) diameter
Corrugated cardboard
Medium-weight card
White covering paper
12×45cm (4¾×18in) medium-weight cotton-type fabric (as the dressing table)
14cm (5½in) circle of pink babycord (or alternative fabric)
45cm (½yd) white lace, preferably 30mm (1–1¼in) deep (as the dressing table)
10×20cm (4×8in) medium-weight polyester wadding
25cm (10in) Antique Blue feather-edge satin ribbon, 10mm (⅜in) wide
1.20m (1¼yd) pink satin ribbon, 1.5mm (¹⁄₁₆in) wide
OR 30cm (12in) very narrow matching braid
Clear adhesive

1. Either cut down a canister to the measurements shown above, or make a cylinder from scrap paper. Cover with white paper.

2. Join the two short edges of the fabric for the skirt, and press the seam open. Mark the top edge equally into eight, then gather 1cm (⅜in) below the edge. Mark the top edge of the cylinder into eight, then pin the skirt round, matching the marked points. Draw up the gathers to fit around the top of the cylinder, then turn the overlapping fabric over the edge and glue down inside. Turn up the hem and stitch. Trim the skirt with lace, lower edges level.

3. Cut two 8cm (3¼in) diameter circles of card for the seat. Glue each to a piece of corrugated cardboard: trim the cardboard level with the card circles. Glue the circles together, the corrugated board sandwiched inside with the ridges running in opposite directions – at right-angles.

4. Cut two 8cm (3¼in) circles of wadding and glue lightly to the top side of the seat.

5. Cut a 14cm (5½in) diameter circle of babycord or alternative fabric. Gather all round the edge, then place the fabric right side down: lower the card circle, wadding side down, into the centre and draw up the gathers tightly underneath the seat, so that it is smoothly covered. Glue on top of the base.

6. Plait three 36cm (15in) lengths of narrow ribbon to make braid (as chapter 2): glue on top of the skirt gathers.

7. Make a bow (method A in chapter 2) from 10cm (4in) of feather-edge ribbon, with streamers made from 15cm (6in). Stitch to the back of the stool, as illustrated. Trim the cut ends in an inverted V-shape.

PEARL-FRAMED DRESSING TABLE MIRROR

*A*n oval mirror edged with pearls is *perfect for the draped dressing table, but you could adapt any small rectangular mirror – just frame it with braid. However, it is easy to alter the shape by setting it in an oval frame, as illustrated: if you prefer a different shape, simply change the design accordingly. If your mirror is a little larger or smaller, check it against the pattern and adjust the size as necessary.*

– MATERIALS –

Purse mirror, 8×6cm (3×2½in)
12×25cm (5×10in) stiff pale blue paper
3×14.5cm (1¼×5¾in) thin card
3m (3yd) Antique Blue satin ribbon, 1.5mm (¹⁄₁₆in) wide
OR 40cm (½yd) fold-over lampshade braid, 10mm (⅜in) wide
12cm (5in) Rosy Mauve single-face satin ribbon, 6mm (¼in) wide
30cm (12in) pearl trim
25cm (10in) pearl trim with fabric edge (if unavailable, pearl trim as above)
Clear adhesive

---

1. Cut the pattern twice in coloured paper: cut out the centre oval on one piece only, for the front. Glue the fabric edge of the pearls to the back of this piece, so the pearls edge the oval (if no fabric edge, glue the pearls to the edge of the paper, on the right side).

2. Place the mirror between the two pieces of paper and glue the edges together.

3. Cut the ribbon in half and make two lengths of plaited braid (as chapter 2). Beginning and ending at the centre top, glue one all round the outer edge of the front: repeat on the back; or glue braid all round the edge, folding it neatly over. Glue pearls around the sides and

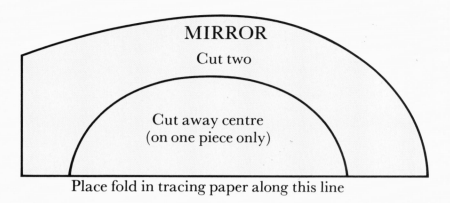

MIRROR

Cut two

Cut away centre
(on one piece only)

Place fold in tracing paper along this line

| B | Cut one | Base | STRUT (Mirror) | A |

PEARL-FRAMED DRESSING TABLE MIRROR

top, between the plaited ribbon or over the fold in the braid. Make a rose (see chapter 2) from the pink ribbon, and glue it at the top, over join in braid.

4. Cut the strut as pattern in thin card and score the broken lines. Cover one large section with coloured paper. Bend round and glue tab A behind B. Glue to the back of the mirror.

POWDER-PUFF AND PINCUSHION

I *mportant accessories for any girl's dressing table, these add touches of soft pink to echo the colour scheme.*

– MATERIALS –

6×10cm (2½×4in) deep pink felt
Pink cotton-wool ball
25cm (10in) pale pink lace, 10mm (⅜in) deep

12cm (5in) feather-edge Rosy Mauve satin ribbon, 9mm (⅜in) wide
Polyester stuffing (or scraps of wadding)
Medium-weight card
Clear adhesive

————— · —————

1. Cut the top of the pincushion once in felt, and the base twice in card. Glue the two pieces of card together, then glue them onto felt and cut the felt about 2mm (¹⁄₁₆in) outside the card (as broken line).

2. Mark the edge of the felt circle equally into four, then gather close to the edge. Mark the base into four, then pin the two circles together, card inside, matching the marked points. Draw up to fit and oversew together, distributing the gathers evenly: leave one-quarter open for stuffing. Stuff firmly and close the seam.

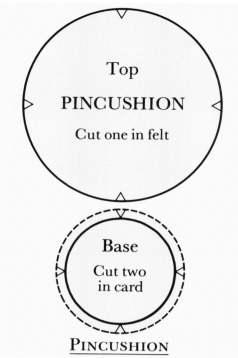

Top

PINCUSHION

Cut one in felt

Base

Cut two in card

PINCUSHION

3. Join the cut ends of the lace to form a circle, then mark into four and gather the straight edge. Pin evenly round the base, then draw up to fit and stitch into place.

4. For the powder-puff, make a bow (as method B in chapter 2) from the ribbon, and glue it on top of the cotton-wool ball.

CURTAINED WARDROBE WITH BOTTOM DRAWER

*P*lenty of hanging space is essential when you have so many clothes to store away. The girls love their elegant wardrobe with its draped curtain and matching padded hangers (see chapter 10). It even has an inner bottom drawer, which is ideal for mob caps, shawls, purses and other bits and bobs – until they have reason to put it to another, more important use!

The wardrobe consists of a corrugated cardboard carton standing on cotton reels: so you shouldn't have too many doubts about whether you can make it. Cover it with a length of left-over wallpaper or some plain-coloured cartridge-weight paper. Or you could use a prettily patterned gift wrap: but in this case cover the surface first with a layer of lining paper.

— MATERIALS —

Corrugated cardboard
Wallpaper or suitable covering paper
3m (3½yd) furnishing braid, 10mm (⅜in) wide
Silk bobble, large bead or round button for drawer knob
45×40cm (18×16in) flowered medium-weight fabric
60cm (¾yd) feather-edge satin ribbon 10mm (⅜in) wide
50cm (½yd) satin ribbon, 1.5mm (1/16in) wide
85cm (1yd) silky lampshade fringe, 25mm (1in) deep
11 small curtain rings (15mm/⅝in)
2 cotton reels
45cm (18in) wooden dowelling, 5mm (¼in) diameter
Short pins: 15mm (⅝in) if available, otherwise 25mm (1in)
Wallpaper paste
Latex adhesive
Clear adhesive

1. Cut one back, two sides and the top and bottom of the wardrobe from corrugated cardboard (ridges as direction of arrows) as dimensions indicated on pattern diagrams. Score the broken lines.

2. Bend back the top tabs *a* and glue into position *between* the two side pieces, as indicated. Glue the bottom between the sides in the same way. Bend all four tabs *b* and glue the back over them. Cover this box inside and out with wallpaper, trimming it level with the front edge (wallpaper paste may not adhere if the outside of the box has been damp-proofed).

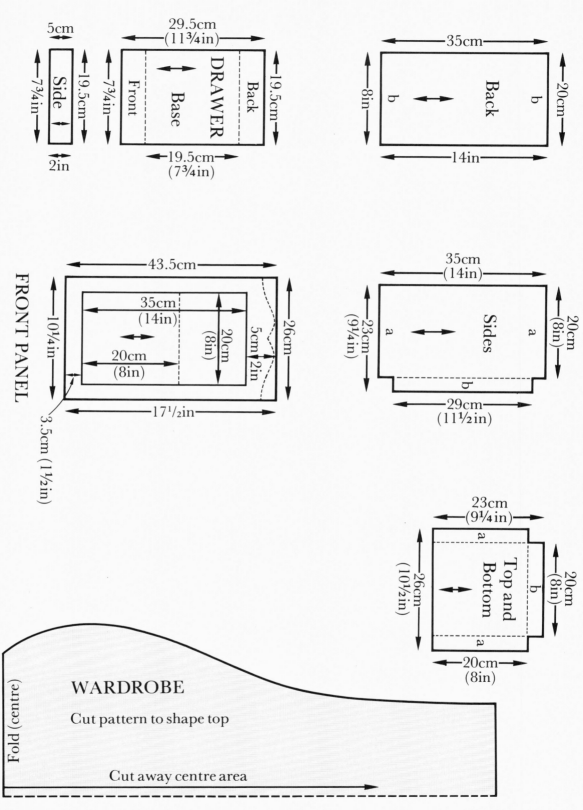

5cm

29.5cm
(11¾in)

DRAWER

Back

Base

Front

19.5cm

7¾in

7¾in

19.5cm

Side

2in

19.5cm
(7¾in)

35cm

Back

b

b

8in

20cm

14in

FRONT PANEL

43.5cm

10¼in

35cm
(14in)

20cm
(8in)

20cm
(8in)

5cm
2in

26cm

17½in

3.5cm (1½in)

35cm
(14in)

Sides

a

a

23cm
(9¼in)

20cm
(8in)

29cm
(11½in)

b

23cm
(9¼in)

Top and
Bottom

a

b

a

26cm
(10½in)

20cm
(8in)

20cm
(8in)

WARDROBE

Cut pattern to shape top

Fold (centre)

Cut away centre area

CURTAINED WARDROBE WITH BOTTOM DRAWER

3. For the drawer, cut one piece for the base and two for the sides, as dimensions given on pattern diagram. Bend the back and front up, then glue the sides between. Cover inside and outside with wallpaper, trimming it level with the top edge.

4. Cut a piece of board for the front panel as dimensions given, shaping the top as shown (trace the pattern and use it as a template): cut out the centre. Glue this piece to another sheet of board, and cut it level with the first piece. Cover the back of this panel with wallpaper, trimming it level with the cut edges. Cover the front also, but allow an extra 3cm (1¼in) to overlap the lower edge, and when cutting away the centre paper, *cut only along the top and sides.* Then cut off the top section as the broken line, leaving a 20cm (8in) square of paper below.

5. Place the front panel over the 'box' and very carefully anchor it in position along the top and sides with tiny pins pushed through the front panel into the thickness of the box. When it is held in place, turn the wardrobe over, front panel down, and glue 3cm (1¼in) wide strips of wallpaper, folded in half lengthways, behind this join, to hold it securely along all *four* edges.

6. Turn under the surplus along the lower edge of the front and stick it to the back of the panel. And glue the loose flap of wallpaper smoothly inside the bottom of the wardrobe. Glue a cotton reel underneath at each back corner: add circles of card underneath if necessary to correct the level.

7. Glue braid over the outer and inner *cut* edges of the front panel (not the lower edges), and also around the top edge of the drawer (have the overlap at the sides and back *inside* the drawer). Fix a bobble, bead or button at centre front of the drawer for the knob.

8. Cut a piece of fabric 45cm (18in) long × 40cm (16in) wide for the curtain. Make a narrow hem along both sides. Turn under the raw top edge, then turn under a 1.5cm (½in) hem and stitch. Gather close above this line of hem-stitching and draw up to measure 20cm (8in). Distribute the gathers evenly and stitch 1.5mm (¹⁄₁₆in) wide ribbon over them on the wrong side to hold in place. Stitch curtain rings to the ribbon at 2cm (¾in) intervals.

9. Cut two 22cm (8½in) lengths of dowelling. Make a hole at each side of the box halfway between the front and back and 2cm (¾in) from the top. Fit one rod through these holes and glue into place. Make two more holes in the sides, 1cm (⅜in) from the front and 1cm (⅜in) from the top.

Slip the second rod through the curtain rings, then fix in position as the previous one. Turn up and stitch the hem. Stitch fringe down the right-hand edge and over the hem. (If necessary, weight the corners to help the curtain hang well – two coins are often cheaper than lead weights!)

10. Make a loop from 22cm (9in) feather-edge ribbon for the tie-back, and fix the cut ends with tiny pins to the back of the front panel, at the left side, 20cm (8in) above the bottom edge. Fold a 15cm (6in) length of ribbon in half for the bow ends, and stitch to the loop at the point where the bow will be positioned. Make a bow from 10cm (4in) ribbon bound with 2cm (¾in) (as method A in chapter 2), and stitch into place. Use the remaining ribbon to make a similar bow, and glue it at the centre top of the front panel. Plait narrow ribbon (as chapter 2) and glue along the centre of the front section of the tie-back loop.

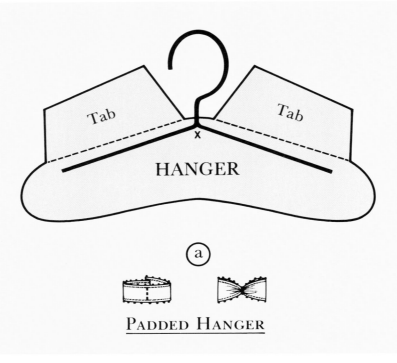

COVERED HANGERS

*T*he hangers illustrated in chapter 10 are
covered with the babycord fabric used
to upholster the chair and dressing table
stool. But you could use any firm, not-too
thin fabric or, of course, felt. And you could
make your own braid from plaited ribbon, as
you did to trim the tie-back on the wardrobe.
The following materials are for one covered
hanger.

– MATERIALS –

Thin card
10cm (4in) square of babycord (or alternative
   fabric)
Pipe cleaner or chenille stem, 16.5cm (6½in)
   long
25cm (10in) narrow silky lampshade braid
6cm (2½in) feather-edge satin ribbon, 10mm
   (⅜in) wide (or other trim)
Thread to match ribbon
Clear adhesive

————— · —————

1. Cut the outline once in card as
pattern, with tabs: and once following the
broken lines, to omit the tabs. Score
broken lines on the first piece.

2. Cover both pieces on one side with
fabric, ignoring the tabs.

3. Bend a pipe cleaner in half to make
it double thickness, then bend it into
shape as the heavy lines on the pattern:
twist at the cross before dividing the
ends. Place on the back of the first piece
of card, as indicated, then bring the tabs
down and glue them over the pipe
cleaner. Glue the second piece on top.

4. Glue braid all round over the cut
edges.

5. Fold the cut ends of the ribbon
back so that they overlap behind the
centre of the ribbon. Gather centre as
broken line (diagram (a)): draw up and
bind tightly with matching thread, then
stitch at the centre of the hanger.

CHAPTER 14

SELLING YOUR KATE GREENAWAY DOLLS

Making dolls isn't just fun. It can give you a lot of creative satisfaction, and be financially rewarding, too: but only if you go about it in the right way. The profits are not great, but with good organisation and careful planning, it can be an enjoyable way to make some extra money. Obviously, the quality of your work must be good enough – or you wouldn't be considering selling it. But that isn't quite enough. You also need a professional approach.

In order to be businesslike right from the start, you need to work out your entire sales strategy before you even think about threading a needle. Begin with some market research. Manufacturers of consumer products all do extensive market research before launching new products, so it can't be a bad idea! They study the market to try to find out exactly what the public likes and wants, so that they don't waste time and money creating a product for which there is no popular demand. You can do exactly the same thing for your dolls.

MARKET RESEARCH

First look around to see who your customers might be: then try to discover exactly what they want. You might find that you can make your dolls to special order: this means that each one could be exclusive and completely individual. Just imagine how thrilled a little girl would be to have her doll wearing a dress to match her own – and perhaps with hair just like hers as well. (Then, of course, all her friends will want a personalised doll too!)

There might be a shop near you that would be happy to take a small number of dolls, so that you wouldn't have the trouble of selling each one separately. This means you could 'mass-produce' them, which speeds things up quite a bit. But remember that the shop will have to add a considerable mark-up to cover its overheads, which reduces the amount you will earn if the final price-tag on the doll is to remain competitive. Ideally, it is better to find your own 'retail outlets' if you possibly can, because the profit margin must obviously be greater. One very satisfactory alternative is a local market: find out if there is one near you through which you could sell your work. The Women's Institute has an excellent scheme which they will be happy to tell you about.

The more people who see your work, the better: so don't pretend you're a blushing violet hiding behind a tree! Be proud of your dolls: you have something attractive to show, and something worthwhile to offer, so tell the world about it! Just a few friends will do for a start: other mothers at playgroup or school, friends or neighbours who work in a nearby factory or office block, fellow members of a club or group, local shop assistants who know you well. Even your friendly neighbourhood milkman! It's amazing how word gets around, and you may soon find you are receiving enquiries from all kinds of unexpected sources.

WHAT KIND OF DOLL?

Remember, you're not even trying to sell your dolls yet. All this initial enquiry is in the cause of market research: having found out who might buy your dolls, ask the sort of questions that will determine the kind of doll you are going to make. Also, get an idea of what it will cost. This is very important! Costing and pricing the finished product is dealt with later, but you must have it in mind from the moment you begin planning. You will, of course, have made up at least one doll so that you can show people what your enterprise is all about. But don't be afraid to discuss adaptations of the original: just don't forget to adapt the price too.

The Kate Greenaway doll, for instance, would make a lovely bride or bridesmaid – either as a present for a romantic little girl or dressed in the actual fabric used for a wedding, as a memento for the bride herself or a small bridesmaid. Make up the basic Kate Greenaway dress (in chapter 6) in the bridal fabric, add a veil with a suitable headdress and give her a posy to hold. Nightdress cases are another popular item. All you need to do is omit the legs, then make the doll's skirt much longer and wider, with a large 'petticoat bag' underneath to hold the nightwear: either make an opening at the centre back of the bag, or insert a zip fastener across the bottom. The possibilities for adaptation are endless once you let your imagination get to work.

PLAN AHEAD FOR CHRISTMAS

Bear in mind that your biggest selling period will be Christmas. And it's not too early to start preparing for it in June or July! Every year the shops warn us to shop early for Christmas: now it's your turn to advise your customers to do the same. The more time you have to work on your orders, the more you will be able to complete, and there will always be a few last-minute ones to ensure you *still*

have to burn the midnight oil.

The Kate Greenaway doll makes a very special Christmas present for a little girl (and for quite a few bigger ones too!), but you might think about designing a doll especially *for* Christmas. Imagine Louisa's Winter Cloak, Bonnet and Muff (chapter 5) made up Santa Claus-style in scarlet felt trimmed with white fur; or the basic Kate Greenaway dress (chapter 6) made up in palest pink, with a gathered net overskirt garlanded with tinsel, a pair of lace-edged wings, some silver sequin stars in her hair and a coronet of flowers – the prettiest Sugar Plum Fairy ever.

SHOPPING AROUND

Once you have decided who your customers are likely to be, and what you think they will want, you are ready for the next step in your plan of campaign. Sit down with a pencil and paper and work out your shopping list. Take your time and make sure you have written down everything you will need, in the correct amounts. It is important to avoid several trips to town when one would do. Saving time is always your primary consideration, but in this case you will be saving money too. It's all too easy to forget the incidental expenses like fares, telephone calls, stationery and postage. A small cash book is essential to keep a note of everything you spend. Without a complete record of your outgoings, you won't be able to cost your work accurately.

Two other essentials are a diary and an address book. The first keeps a note of when you received an order, and the delivery date (appropriately ticked off when you meet it); the second is vital to record all your contacts, customers, suppliers and so on. Jot down the name and telephone extension of the person you deal with in a big organisation.

When you are buying felt, fur fabrics and similar materials for soft toys, you can often get very good bargains from mail order companies, but do try to

choose the pretty fabrics for the Kate Greenaway dresses personally, if you possibly can. Look for inexpensive dress fabrics: the amounts you need are so small that it isn't really possible to buy in bulk. A list of recommended stockists and suppliers of materials is given in chapter 15. Look also at the small ads in the popular women's magazines (particularly those specialising in needlecrafts) for likely names and addresses.

Never miss a sale or a market. Out-of-season dress fabrics may be reduced for clearance. And you can often find very good bargains in lace and other trimmings on market stalls. It is also worth keeping an eye open for inexpensive lace on the shelves of your favourite store. Lace edging varies considerably in price, and you may find one which is perfectly suitable but much cheaper than most of the others. When you do, it's a good idea to lay in a stock for future use.

Back home with all your bags and parcels, have a cup of tea while you check which patterns you are going to need. Bosses and unions agree that regular tea and coffee breaks are essential for happy workers and efficient output, so never feel guilty about stopping for a cup of tea or a mug of coffee: just keep it well away from your work. Get into the habit of putting your reviving brew on a separate table or shelf, or pull up a chair and rest a tray on that. There's nothing more discouraging than a disastrous spill which ruins hours of painstaking work! It can happen to anyone – but it's awful when it does.

GETTING DOWN TO WORK

Ordinary greaseproof paper is fine for doll-makers who will be using their patterns only a few times. But you will need them over and over again, so it is well worth tracing and drawing them onto thin non-woven interlining (Vilene), which is very durable and will avoid the necessity for constant retracing. Transfer all the markings with a fibre-tipped pen,

and don't forget to add the name of the garment to each pattern piece, for quick identification if the pieces ever become muddled. Invent a 'filing system' for your patterns. Slip each set into a small transparent bag, clearly labelled: then keep together in an envelope-type office folder.

Cutting out always tends to be a bit tedious and takes longer than one expects, and it's a great temptation to try to hurry things up a bit. One way is to cut out several pieces at a time, which sounds a great idea in theory, but doesn't always work out so well in practice. Clothing manufacturers do this very successfully: but they are cutting out large pieces with special shears. The Kate Greenaway pattern pieces are tiny in comparison, and if you lose the very precise detail, you can easily ruin the finished garment. And this applies even more to the felt shapes to make the doll itself. So do be patient and spend time on careful cutting out: you may well find you can do two at a time, but more than that can be dangerous, and it isn't worth taking the risk.

AN EYE ON THE CLOCK

It may seem to have taken a long time to reach the stage where you actually start to sew, but you will find that careful preliminary organisation is an essential part of a streamlined operation – and it does get quicker every time. Once you are actually making the dolls you have to keep reminding yourself that as Chairman and Managing Director of your own company, your industrial slogan must be: time is money! Never save time by cutting corners and lowering your usual high standards, but try to avoid time-consuming operations in favour of quicker alternatives.

For instance, it's much easier to trim a dress with flat lace than if you have to gather it. When you are selecting an outfit, don't choose one which has a lot of complicated detail. For example, only make Emily's Old-fashioned Ballgown

(chapter 10) for a special customer who is prepared to pay a price that reflects the amount of work in it. But outfits like those worn by Louisa and Charlotte in the winter scene in chapter 9 are equally spectacular, yet wonderfully quick to make: in the case of Charlotte's coat, you might decide to save time with a purchased braid, and just trim her hat with a broad band of ribbon and a big bow.

Consider your trimmings very carefully, remembering that time is money. If you study the photographs in this book, you will see that it is often the trimmings that 'make' a garment, especially on a plain fabric. But one broad band of lace might be no more expensive than three narrow ones, and would take a third of the time to sew. Bought braid is quicker than making it yourself. And if you're making tiny bows, method B in chapter 2 is much quicker than method A.

You could save even more time and expense by finding a patterned fabric with an all-over design which needs even less trimming. Examples of this are shown in chapter 6 (Improving Occupations). The typically Kate Greenaway printed shift dresses are absolutely basic, very quick and easy to make. You can save yet more time by omitting the braid trim – just take the lace up to cover *all* the bias binding. Notice their shoes, too: little bows are quicker for you than roses. The results of all this 'streamlining' will be just as attractive as some of the other designs which have far more work in them. Leave those for the reader who is making the doll for fun: *your* aim is minimum work for maximum output!

'Mini' Mass-production

If you manage to find a market that allows you to 'mass-produce' your dolls, you will find it speeds up production considerably. But don't be too ambitious: doing the same operation over and *over* again can become very tedious indeed. Six at a time is probably the most

practical number to attempt, with an absolute limit of ten (don't forget this means *twenty* arms and *twenty* legs). Over that number boredom sets in at an alarming rate – and you're in danger of developing a severe allergy to anything that even looks like a doll!

It is tremendously important that you should never lose your enthusiasm. When you cease to enjoy your doll-making and it becomes a chore – that is the time to stop. If you don't mind being bored to tears, then there are far more lucrative ways to make money. Your dolls must always remain a pleasure: because, unfortunately, the creative satisfaction will inevitably be greater than the financial rewards.

It helps to have a tidy mind to organise your 'mini' mass-production. But if you're not naturally tidy-minded, make a big effort and have lots of small boxes and trays into which you can sort the separate bits and pieces – from disembodied limbs to measured lengths of lace and ribbon, elastic, snap fasteners and so on. Use large grocery boxes to store half-made dolls and fabrics and collect polystyrene trays, yoghurt pots and other cartons from the supermarket to hold smaller items. There's so much disposable packaging these days, you'll never be at a loss for suitable pigeon-holes: only your dustbin will be the loser!

Presentation

When your dolls are finished they will, of course, be very special. So they deserve some special treatment. The Kate Greenaway designer label (see below) gives them a professional appearance, that 'touch of class' which is so valuable when you are selling your work. But attractive packaging is very important too: not only is it essential to protect the doll, it also makes her look very special. A smart box is the ideal form of packaging, but it is usually too expensive to be practicable: the best compromise is to

make your own 'lid-less' box from plain card and then fill it with white or pastel-coloured tissue paper. When the doll is nestled inside and looking very precious, cover the whole thing with cling-film, sealing it underneath. But making boxes takes valuable time, and you may prefer to settle for a good-quality see-through bag: in this case, your doll will look twice as attractive if you fix her to a piece of card before sealing her inside.

PRICING, TAX AND PUBLICITY

Last, but not least, the subject that worries everyone – pricing your product. This is the most difficult part of the whole operation, but it's the stage when you must be at your most professional. And it's the reason why it is vital to be efficiently organised right from the beginning and have a special cash book into which you enter every penny you spend on materials and other expenses. Only by doing this can you calculate how much the doll has actually cost you to make. To this you must add what you feel your time is worth. The sad fact here is that if you add too accurate an assessment of what your work is really worth, your doll will be so highly priced that it won't sell, however beautiful it is. So to be competitive, you have to undervalue yourself and try to derive some consolation from the fact that at least you have enjoyed doing it.

Remember, it is essential to cost out your doll as accurately as possible, and then decide how much 'profit' you are going to add *before* you begin to make the dolls you plan to sell. If you are making dolls to order, you will of course have to do so, in order to fix a price with your customer. But even if you are making the dolls with the intention of selling them afterwards, it is still just as important to know the exact price you are aiming to charge, to ensure that it is both practicable and competitive.

Depending on your present income, and how many dolls you sell, you may have to pay income tax on your additional earnings. Contact your local tax inspector at the outset if you are worried about your tax position, or ask him or her for help in filling in your tax return.

There are various safety regulations that apply to soft toys that you need to comply with. They must not be made from materials that are likely to catch fire easily; glass or plastic eyes must be properly fixed; stuffing should be clean; and there should be no metal parts or wires which might protrude. If you make the dolls according to the directions and guidelines set out in this book, they should conform to these regulations.

Finally, take a tip from all those manufacturers of soap powder, chocolate etc. Never underestimate the power of advertising. In your own case, *your work is your best advertisement*. All you need to spread the word is that all-important Kate Greenaway label.

THE KATE GREENAWAY DOLL DESIGNER LABELS

Here are your Kate Greenaway doll designer labels. Cut out, stick onto card, and use them with pride. Further supplies (uncoloured) may be obtained from: Valerie Janitch, 15 Ledway Drive, Wembley Park, Middlesex HA9 9TH. Please enclose £1.00 (for 48 labels): postage and packing is inclusive.

To maintain a high quality of individual craftsmanship, and to ensure that the Kate Greenaway doll remains an exclusive design only for the personal use of readers of this book, orders are limited to 48 labels per person in any six-month period. This offer is regrettably only open to readers in the United Kingdom and Northern Ireland.

Details of other books and patterns by Valerie Janitch can be obtained from the above address. Just send a stamped self-addressed envelope.

CHAPTER 15

RECOMMENDED STOCKISTS AND SUPPLIERS

You will find an excellent selection of fabrics at all branches of the John Lewis Partnership (UK). They also stock a wide range of lace edgings, braids, knitting yarns, felt, polyester stuffing, interlining, wadding, embroidery cottons, sequins and other trimmings, as well as all general sewing equipment and adhesives.

Offray ribbons can be found in good needlework and craft shops throughout the UK and the US, as well as in many large department stores, including D. H. Evans, Oxford Street, London, W1A 1DE and all other House of Fraser stores (for your nearest stockist write to: C. M. Offray and Son Ltd, Fir Tree Place, Church Road, Ashford, Middlesex TW15 2PH).

Turned paper balls (eg for Louisa's Birthday Doll) can be obtained from most good craft shops. In case of difficulty, The Handicraft Shop, Northgate, Canterbury, CT1 1BE, operates an excellent mail order service (write, or telephone 0227 451188). They also stock felt, chenille stems, adhesives and Offray ribbons.

The Wedgwood china illustrated in chapters 4, 5 and 8 is also from John Lewis, Oxford Street, London W1A 1EX.

This is
_____
a Kate Greenaway doll
designed by Valerie Janitch
and hand-made in

_____
by
_____

This is
_____
a Kate Greenaway doll
designed by Valerie Janitch
and hand-made in

_____
by
_____

This is
_____
a Kate Greenaway doll
designed by Valerie Janitch
and hand-made in

_____
by
_____

This is
_____
a Kate Greenaway doll
designed by Valerie Janitch
and hand-made in

_____
by
_____

This is
_____
a Kate Greenaway doll
designed by Valerie Janitch
and hand-made in

_____
by
_____

This is
_____
a Kate Greenaway doll
designed by Valerie Janitch
and hand-made in

_____
by
_____

This is

_____

a Kate Greenaway doll

designed by Valerie Janitch

and hand-made in

_____

by

_____

This is

_____

a Kate Greenaway doll

designed by Valerie Janitch

and hand-made in

_____

by

_____

This is

_____

a Kate Greenaway doll

designed by Valerie Janitch

and hand-made in

_____

by

_____

This is

_____

a Kate Greenaway doll

designed by Valerie Janitch

and hand-made in

_____

by

_____

This is

_____

a Kate Greenaway doll

designed by Valerie Janitch

and hand-made in

_____

by

_____

This is

_____

a Kate Greenaway doll

designed by Valerie Janitch

and hand-made in

_____

by

_____